Start Investing with Small Income

Start Investing with Small Income

Simple strategies to build wealth from paychecks, side hustles, or gig income

Leah Wynford

Mindful Pages

Published in 2025

ISBN: 9789371773706 (PB)
ISBN: 9789371773645 (eBook)

Published by

Mindful Pages
Imprint of Alpha Editions LLC
312 W. 2nd St #1834
Casper, WY 82601, USA

This book was developed using advanced writing tools to support the drafting and ideation process. All content has been thoughtfully curated, refined, and reviewed to ensure quality and relevance.

Content

Introduction
Investing as a Form of Self-Respect

Investing has often been portrayed as a pursuit reserved for those with ample resources—an arena dominated by vast sums, insider knowledge, and exclusive networks. Start Investing with Small Income confronts this misconception directly. It is not a handbook for rapid wealth or speculative gambles promising instant results. Rather, it asserts a fundamental truth: investing, even in modest increments, is an act of profound self-respect and personal agency. Each decision to allocate resources, however small, is a conscious step toward reclaiming dignity and shaping a future of financial possibility despite present limitations.

Why does this matter? For millions living on limited or irregular incomes—whether from gig work, part-time employment, or modest salaries—conventional financial advice often feels irrelevant. Most literature assumes disposable income, stable employment, or unfettered access to credit. Such assumptions obscure the reality where every pound must be stretched, errors carry weighty consequences, and the mental burden of scarcity colours every decision. This book refuses to ignore that reality; it places it front and centre.

Investing on a modest income is, in itself, a quiet rebellion against a deeply ingrained narrative: that small sums are insignificant, that wealth must be monumental to matter, and that systemic barriers are insurmountable. Too often, people are told they must "earn more first" or "save extensively" before investing. Here, the narrative flips. Wealth begins not with external accumulation but as an internal process—a transformation of identity and belief. Investment becomes less about the size of today's wallet and more about the story one tells oneself: that growth, endurance, and careful stewardship are possible even under constraints.

Even an investment as small as £5 carries symbolic and practical significance. It declares faith in the future self, an assertion that despite systemic hurdles and cultural messages of scarcity, one has the agency to participate in tomorrow's economy. These micro-investments are seeds planted in fallow ground, each with the potential to grow momentum over time. More importantly, they yield emotional returns: pride, confidence, and the quiet courage to continue.

The book maintains a sharp focus on the emotional and behavioural dynamics that shape financial choices for low-income earners. Investing is never purely transactional; it exists within layers of fear, hope, cultural legacy, and psychological resistance. Many readers will recognise the frustration of advice that feels abstract or out of touch—guidance that inadvertently magnifies feelings of inadequacy. In contrast, this book offers an empathetic approach, grounded in lived experience, equipping readers with practical tools designed for immediate, actionable use.

Financial resilience is reframed here as stewardship rather than mere survival. Budgeting and saving are presented not as restrictive chores but as narrative acts aligning daily choices with broader goals. The book introduces the notion of Emotional Return on Investment, illustrating how small financial acts yield essential, intangible benefits in self-trust and agency. It also addresses the psychology of thresholds: progressing from £5 to £50, then to £500, is as much a journey of mindset and habit as it is a financial one.

Technology and innovation are embraced as accessible allies rather than exclusive privileges. Fractional shares, automated investing, and low-minimum platforms are positioned as tools for habit formation and consistent practice, designed to work with the unpredictability of variable incomes. Guidance balances realism with optimism, urging patience while validating the very real challenges readers face.

The urgency of this message lies in the often-overlooked power of incremental change. There is a pervasive myth that financial empowerment requires grand gestures or perfect conditions. Yet experience and behavioural science alike show that small, consistent actions compound into meaningful transformation. Time, rather than income alone, becomes the most democratic force in investing—and this book encourages readers to harness it without waiting for ideal circumstances.

What emerges here is as much a philosophy as a strategy. Wealth begins in the mind and heart, not at the bank. By inviting readers to author their own financial story, to move beyond scarcity conditioning, and to ritualise investment as a facet of identity, the book offers a pathway that is simultaneously accessible and transformative. It acknowledges complexity yet resists despair, presenting a vision in which financial self-respect is practised daily, regardless of income.

This is a quiet revolution. It challenges the assumption that economic systems dictate worth and instead insists on the possibility of self-determination through deliberate, meaningful investment—even when sums appear small. Persistence, clarity, and belief become the guiding principles.

As readers engage with these pages, they are encouraged to confront and reframe familiar assumptions, translating modest financial acts into sustained momentum. The chapters ahead combine philosophical insight with practical guidance, honouring current realities while expanding visions of what is possible.

By choosing to invest, however incrementally, readers claim a future that respects their dignity and potential. This book serves both as map and companion on the journey from survival to stewardship, from scarcity to agency. In this light, investing is elevated beyond a mere financial transaction—it becomes an enduring expression of self-respect.

Chapter 1
Before the First Dollar—Redefining Wealth on Your Terms

At the core of personal finance lies a persistent myth—one that quietly shapes how millions perceive money long before they ever open a bank statement or review an investment portfolio. This myth murmurs that without abundance, one is powerless; that small sums are meaningless; that wealth belongs only to those already well-endowed. It is a legacy of scarcity conditioning, a cultural inheritance that affects not only economic circumstances but also the emotions and identities intertwined with financial self-worth. To embark on investing with a modest income, one must first confront and dismantle this falsehood. Before a single pound is saved or invested, a recalibration is required—a redefinition of wealth that emphasises self-trust, stewardship, and personal agency over mere accumulation.

Scarcity conditioning is more than an economic fact; it is a psychological architecture built through repeated experiences of insufficiency, reinforced by societal narratives. The message "you don't have enough" imposes an emotional burden—a weight of shame, anxiety, and resignation that suppresses initiative and discourages risk-taking. Traditional advice assumes a starting point of surplus or at least disposable income. For those living paycheck to paycheck, such frameworks feel alien, even exclusionary. The challenge is not merely access to capital but navigating the dissonance of being told that what little one can spare is too trivial to matter.

Yet small sums carry power, though rarely in their immediate purchasing ability. Their significance lies in symbolism—the beginning of a narrative shift. Wealth, then, is understood not as a fixed product but as an ongoing process: cultivating self-trust, practising patience, and steadily building momentum through deliberate, consistent acts. Every financial decision, however modest, contributes to shaping an investor's identity and potential. The lie that "not enough" equals "no impact" must be rejected; small money is potent because it initiates agency.

Traditional financial guidance often leaves low-income earners behind due to underlying assumptions. It presumes steady employment, predictable expenses, and surplus funds for saving or investment. Budgeting advice frequently relies on linear timelines and standardised categories. Investment strategies assume scale—minimum deposits, diversification thresholds, and risk allocations calibrated for those with financial cushions. Such frameworks overlook the volatility of gig work, side hustles, and the daily trade-offs faced by those navigating precarious circumstances.

More fundamentally, mainstream advice frames money management as a transactional pipeline: earn more, spend less, invest the remainder. In practice, when every penny counts toward essentials—food, rent, utilities—decisions are rarely discretionary. This is not merely a relevance gap; it is an empathy gap. Financial stability for many is a precarious balancing act, not a straightforward path toward investing readiness.

Transitioning from survival to stewardship is a conceptual shift central to this chapter. Survival implies reactive behaviour—scrambling to meet immediate needs, responding to crises, viewing money as fleeting. Stewardship reframes decisions as deliberate acts of care and vision, even amid scarcity. Every pound, every small investment, becomes an opportunity to nurture growth and resilience. Financial empowerment is understood not as a sudden arrival but as a practice cultivated incrementally.

This reframing positions readers as active custodians rather than passive recipients. Saving, budgeting, or investing—even in tiny amounts—becomes a declaration of stewardship, signalling a shift from scarcity to possibility, from fear to intention.

Central to this philosophy is the notion of Emotional Return on Investment (Emotional ROI), redefining success for those with limited means. Conventional metrics emphasise numerical growth or portfolio value. Emotional ROI prioritises the intangible yet essential gains: agency, pride, and inner momentum. The act of investing—even seemingly insignificant sums—cultivates control and forward orientation that transcend immediate monetary worth.

Emotional ROI recognises investing as a psychological as well as financial practice. Putting aside £5, for example, reinforces self-efficacy—the conviction that one can shape a financial future. This emotional capital builds resilience against discouragement and sustains ongoing commitment. Investing becomes a lived practice, imbued with meaning, rather than an abstract or intimidating concept.

The implications extend beyond individual psychology, challenging conventional notions of wealth and success. By valuing emotional and behavioural gains, investing becomes accessible to those often sidelined by traditional finance. It promotes a more inclusive narrative—wealth is not a final tally but a process, shaped by consistent, intentional effort.

This chapter lays the philosophical foundation for the entire book, honouring the lived realities of low-income earners while charting a path to empowerment. It calls readers to interrogate inherited beliefs, reject limiting narratives, and adopt a new lens through which to view money and investment. True wealth-building, it asserts, begins not in the bank but in the mind.

Investing with a small income is therefore not an act of compromise but a declaration of dignity and vision. It is a commitment to stewardship over mere survival, cultivating emotional and financial resilience through consistent, intentional steps. Subsequent chapters build on this foundation, offering practical strategies, habit formation, and accessible tools to translate small beginnings into enduring wealth.

By shifting the conversation from scarcity to agency, and from conventional finance to emotional empowerment, this chapter equips readers to take the first crucial step: embracing their capacity to invest before any pound is formally set aside. Wealth begins not in a balance sheet, but in the story we tell ourselves—a story of trust, patience, and possibility.

The Lie of "Not Enough"

Scarcity is a powerful force, not merely in economic terms but as a pervasive mindset that shapes how individuals perceive their worth, their possibilities, and their relationship to money itself. The assertion that one has "not enough" is often accepted as an immutable truth, yet this belief is neither natural nor inevitable. Instead, it is a learned condition—what psychologists and behavioural economists call *scarcity conditioning*—that distorts decision-making, limits vision, and ultimately inhibits financial agency. To challenge this lie is to confront a deeply embedded cultural narrative that equates small amounts of money with insignificance and, by extension, a diminished sense of self. It is a narrative that must be dismantled if investing on a modest income is to be more than a theoretical possibility and instead become a lived reality.

Scarcity conditioning emerges from repeated experiences of lack, often magnified by systemic inequalities, cultural messaging, and the emotional toll of economic hardship. When individuals live under conditions where every pound is contested—where rent, food, and basic needs consume the lion's share of income—the psychological weight of "not enough" becomes a chronic stressor. This stress is not merely the discomfort of financial shortfall but an all-encompassing mental state that narrows attention, elevates anxiety, and fosters a sense of helplessness. Research from behavioural science, notably the work of Sendhil Mullainathan and Eldar Shafir in *Scarcity: Why Having Too Little Means So Much*, shows how scarcity hijacks cognitive bandwidth, forcing people into a short-term focus that impedes planning and self-control. This cognitive toll is a direct assault on the capacity to build wealth over time, as it saps the mental energy required to engage in complex financial tasks like budgeting, saving, or investing.

This emotional and cognitive constriction feeds the lie that small amounts of money are powerless. The cultural story reinforced by mainstream media and even some financial advice channels suggests that meaningful financial progress requires large capital, stable income, or a windfall. Under this influence, the very idea of investing with modest resources appears futile, a quixotic gesture doomed to insignificance. Yet, this is a misunderstanding of what wealth-building entails and, more importantly, what *wealth itself* means. Wealth is commonly defined as an accumulation of assets or net worth, but such a definition ignores the profound internal dynamics that precede external financial gains.

To reconceive wealth is to recognise it as a process of *self-trust* rather than mere accumulation. The act of setting aside even a small sum—whether £5, £10, or £20—holds significance not primarily because of its dollar value but because of what it signals about the investor's relationship with their future self. This process of building trust in one's ability to steward resources cultivates a foundational psychological asset without which financial growth cannot occur. Self-trust is the engine of consistency; it is what transforms disparate actions into a coherent financial identity. Without this internal shift, no amount of money, large or small, can sustainably grow because the behavioural habits required to steward wealth remain absent.

Consider the experience of Sarah, a part-time retail worker supporting her family on a modest income. For years, she believed that her £10 weekly surplus was too trivial to bother investing. Her focus remained fixated on immediate bills and day-to-day survival. However, when introduced to micro-investing platforms that allowed her to start with minimal amounts, Sarah began to view her small contributions as meaningful commitments to herself. Over time, these incremental acts reshaped her relationship with money. The money she invested became less about the returns and more about the *proof* of her capacity to plan, delay gratification, and participate in a system previously perceived as inaccessible. This emotional and behavioural transformation—her growing self-trust—set the stage for further financial engagement and resilience.

This example illuminates a crucial truth: *the power of small money is as much symbolic as it is material.* Symbols shape human behaviour profoundly; they influence belief systems, self-perception, and motivation. By investing even modest sums, individuals declare an intention and enact a vision of themselves as future-oriented and capable stewards. The monetary value is secondary to this internal affirmation. In reframing wealth as self-trust, the emphasis shifts from an external goal to an internal process, one that nurtures the psychological groundwork necessary for sustainable financial growth.

The implications of this reframing challenge the orthodoxies embedded in traditional finance, which often centre on accumulation, portfolio diversification, and maximising returns. These paradigms, while useful at higher income levels, risk alienating those for whom the initial challenge is simply to imagine a future where investing is possible. By focusing instead on emotional and behavioural foundations, this approach acknowledges that wealth-building is first a psychological journey. The lie of "not enough" is dispelled not by immediate financial gains but by the gradual reclamation of agency over one's economic narrative.

Critically, this perspective also demands a reconsideration of cultural narratives around poverty and financial worth. The association of low income with low value is deeply entrenched, reinforced by social stigma and systemic exclusion. Yet, wealth as self-trust asserts that value is inherent and independent of external measures. It recognises that dignity and financial agency are rights rather than rewards. This shift is essential for dismantling barriers that go beyond economics to include psychological and cultural dimensions.

Furthermore, challenging scarcity conditioning invites a more compassionate and realistic understanding of financial behaviour. It explains why traditional advice to "save more" or "invest early" often fails not because of laziness or ignorance but due to the profound mental constraints imposed by scarcity. When every financial decision feels like a high-stakes gamble, small losses or unexpected expenses can derail even the most well-intentioned plans. Acknowledging these realities is vital to designing financial strategies that are both practical and psychologically attuned.

The lie of "not enough" thus functions as both a symptom and a cause of financial exclusion. It perpetuates a cycle where low income breeds low confidence, which in turn inhibits the behaviours necessary for wealth-building, reinforcing economic stagnation. Breaking this cycle requires a deliberate shift in narrative and practice—one that values small sums, prioritises emotional returns, and treats investing as an act of self-respect.

Importantly, this shift does not romanticise poverty or suggest that small money is a panacea. Rather, it situates modest investing within a broader framework of financial empowerment that includes realistic budgeting, saving, and system navigation. It recognises the structural barriers that persist but emphasises that these barriers do not negate individual capacity for agency. Every small investment is a step toward reclaiming control, rewriting the money story inherited from family, community, and culture.

Emerging research in behavioural finance supports this approach. Studies indicate that micro-investing and incremental financial behaviours foster habit formation and increase engagement among lower-income populations. These behaviours promote what some scholars term "financial efficacy," the belief that one can successfully manage finances despite constraints. Financial efficacy is closely linked to better long-term outcomes, demonstrating that the psychological dimensions of investing are as critical as the financial mechanics.

The lie of "not enough" also obscures the collective dimension of wealth. Individual acts of investing, however small, accumulate culturally and communally when shared as stories and practices. When people who previously felt excluded begin to see their efforts as meaningful, it seeds a broader cultural shift that challenges economic gatekeeping and redefines who belongs in the financial ecosystem. This communal redefinition is an essential step toward greater economic inclusion and social equity.

In this light, the act of investing small sums becomes not just a financial transaction but a radical statement of possibility and belonging. It is a rejection of scarcity's psychological grip and an embrace of abundance defined by agency rather than assets. This conceptual reorientation is the foundation upon which the rest of this book builds—a philosophy that honours where readers are today while opening pathways toward where they can be tomorrow.

Reclaiming the power of small money and rejecting the lie of "not enough" requires cultivating patience, discipline, and a long-term perspective. It asks readers to view their financial lives through a lens of growth and identity rather than deficit and limitation. The work is subtle and gradual, but no less profound for it. In embracing this truth, readers can begin to reframe their relationship with money, laying the groundwork for sustained financial engagement and resilience.

Ultimately, the lie of "not enough" is not simply a mistaken belief; it is a barrier to empowerment that can be dismantled through intentional narrative change and practical action. Recognising that wealth is a process of self-trust transforms the challenge of investing on a small income from an impossibility into a meaningful, attainable endeavour. It invites readers to claim their financial agency, not despite their circumstances, but because of a conscious choice to see value where others see scarcity. This redefinition is not merely strategic; it is an act of dignity and vision.

Why Traditional Finance Leaves You Behind

Mainstream financial advice, though widely disseminated and culturally dominant, often serves as an ill-fitting blueprint for those living paycheck to paycheck. At first glance, the principles of budgeting, saving, and investing appear universally applicable—commonsense steps to secure a stable financial future. Yet beneath this veneer of universality lie deep assumptions that render much of this guidance inaccessible, irrelevant, or even counterproductive for individuals with limited, inconsistent, or unpredictable incomes. The disconnect is not merely one of scale but of fundamental design: traditional finance presupposes a starting point and a set of circumstances that many cannot claim. To fully grasp why this advice falls short, it is essential to dissect the implicit premises it carries and to explore how these misalignments create systemic exclusion.

Most financial advice begins with the presumption of *disposable income*—the portion of earnings remaining after essential expenses that can be allocated towards savings or investments. This presumption is rarely stated explicitly but is foundational to conventional strategies. It underpins recommendations to automate transfers, invest a fixed percentage of income, or prioritise debt repayment before investing. For individuals whose monthly budget is consumed by essentials such as rent, utilities, childcare, and food, the concept of disposable income is not merely aspirational; it is frequently nonexistent. According to data from the Resolution Foundation, a significant segment of the UK workforce lives paycheck to paycheck, with negligible or no financial buffer. For these individuals, the traditional financial formula collapses under the weight of lived realities.

Moreover, many budgeting frameworks operate on *predictability and regularity*—assumptions ill-suited to the gig economy, freelance work, or informal side hustles, where income may fluctuate dramatically month to month. The ubiquitous "50/30/20 rule," which suggests allocating 50% of income to necessities, 30% to discretionary spending, and 20% to savings, becomes impractical when earnings vary weekly or daily. This instability demands a budgeting approach that is not linear but dynamic, adaptive to shifting cash flows, and responsive to unpredictability. Yet mainstream advice, largely designed around steady paychecks and fixed expenses, offers few tools tailored to these needs. The result is frustration and a sense of failure when budgets derived from rigid models inevitably crumble under real-world volatility.

Investing advice, similarly, tends to assume not only disposable income but also *access to financial infrastructure and knowledge.* Many traditional investment vehicles require minimum deposits or carry fees that are prohibitive for low-income individuals. Mutual funds, for example, often impose minimum investments of several hundred pounds, placing them beyond reach for those prioritising immediate expenses. Additionally, the language and concepts surrounding investing—risk tolerance, portfolio diversification, asset allocation—can seem esoteric without accessible education or mentorship. This technical complexity compounds feelings of exclusion and undermines confidence. It is telling that, according to recent surveys, low-income groups are disproportionately underrepresented among retail investors. The problem is not disinterest but systemic barriers built into the very architecture of mainstream finance.

This misalignment is not merely a matter of practical inconvenience but one of ethical concern. Financial advice that fails to account for the realities of low-income earners risks perpetuating economic inequality by reinforcing narratives of blame and inadequacy. When advice is framed around ideals that many cannot meet, it inadvertently stigmatizes those who do not conform, attributing their challenges to personal failings rather than structural obstacles. Such framing obscures the role of wage stagnation, rising living costs, and credit access disparities in shaping financial capacity. It also overlooks the psychological toll exacted by persistent financial precarity—stress, cognitive overload, and decision fatigue—that traditional advice rarely addresses.

The inherent inadequacy of conventional financial guidance calls for a paradigmatic shift—a move towards advice that respects and works within constraints rather than ignoring them. This entails recognising that budgeting and investing for those living paycheck to paycheck demand strategies that prioritise *flexibility, resilience, and emotional sustainability*. Budgeting becomes not a rigid plan but a narrative tool that adapts to income variability, focusing on *micro-margins*—the small, deliberate gaps that can be harvested over time rather than dramatic cutbacks. Similarly, investing strategies must be accessible in both cost and complexity, leveraging innovations like fractional shares and automated micro-investing platforms that allow participation at any scale.

Furthermore, this shift requires acknowledging the *emotional and behavioural dimensions* of financial management. Traditional advice often adopts a prescriptive tone, emphasising discipline and sacrifice without addressing the psychological barriers that scarcity imposes. For many, the decision to allocate limited funds to investment rather than immediate consumption involves navigating emotional conflicts—balancing present needs with future aspirations amid uncertainty. Understanding these tensions is crucial to designing advice that not only informs but supports sustainable action.

Real-world examples illustrate how this reorientation can succeed. Platforms like Acorns and Moneybox, which round up everyday purchases to invest spare change, exemplify accessibility by removing minimum thresholds and automating engagement. Such innovations reduce the cognitive burden and psychological friction often associated with investing, offering an entry point for those previously excluded. Additionally, community-based financial education programmes that emphasise peer learning and culturally relevant narratives foster empowerment by demystifying finance and normalising small-scale investing. These models demonstrate that when advice aligns with the lived experiences of low-income earners, it catalyses meaningful participation rather than alienation.

Yet, it is important to recognise that no single strategy offers a panacea. Structural inequalities—unequal access to credit, housing insecurity, labour market volatility—continue to constrain financial options. The failure of traditional advice is symptomatic of broader systemic gaps that require policy interventions alongside individual empowerment. Financial guidance that respects these limitations while equipping readers with practical, scalable tools embodies a pragmatic optimism: it neither glosses over hardship nor resigns itself to it.

This chapter invites readers to critically interrogate the financial advice they encounter, to question assumptions about income, stability, and access, and to reclaim their own frameworks for budgeting and investing. It sets the stage for exploring adaptive strategies tailored to the realities of low and variable incomes—strategies that honour resilience over perfection and incremental progress over immediate transformation. By doing so, it challenges the dominant financial paradigm and opens space for more inclusive, effective pathways toward wealth-building.

Ultimately, understanding why traditional finance leaves so many behind is not merely an intellectual exercise but a prerequisite for designing financial lives that are equitable and sustainable. It reveals that the conventional wisdom is often a reflection of privilege disguised as universality. The task ahead is to replace this narrow lens with one that centres lived experience, embraces complexity, and recognises the nuanced interplay between economic conditions and human behaviour. Only then can financial advice fulfil its promise as a tool for empowerment rather than exclusion.

From Survival to Stewardship

The financial lives of many individuals living on modest or unpredictable incomes are often characterised by a relentless struggle for survival—a state of constant reaction to immediate needs and crises. This survival mode, while understandable and necessary in many respects, narrows the cognitive and emotional bandwidth available to envision and enact long-term financial agency. Yet beneath this surface of urgency and scarcity lies untapped potential for transformation. Shifting from survival to stewardship involves more than just practical budgeting changes; it requires a fundamental reorientation of how financial decisions are understood and experienced. It invites readers to see their daily money choices not as desperate reactions but as deliberate, visionary acts that cultivate control, dignity, and future possibility, regardless of the size of their income.

Survival is often the default mode when resources are limited and pressures are immediate. It compels individuals to prioritise urgent expenses—rent, utilities, food—above all else, creating a cycle where financial planning beyond the next week or month feels both unattainable and irrelevant. This immediacy breeds a scarcity mindset, which behavioural economics has shown constrains not only decisions but also self-perception. People caught in scarcity often perceive their circumstances as fixed, leading to a sense of powerlessness that inhibits proactive financial behaviour. The psychological strain of survival mode reduces capacity for foresight, making the very idea of investing or saving seem disconnected from reality.

However, survival and stewardship need not be mutually exclusive. Stewardship reframes financial management as an ongoing act of care and responsibility—both toward one's present needs and future aspirations. It positions money as a resource to be tended thoughtfully, even when scarce, rather than a mere fuel for short-term reaction. This conceptual shift aligns with contemporary understandings of financial resilience, which emphasise adaptability, intention, and incremental progress. Stewardship is not about having abundance but about exercising agency within constraints, recognising that every financial choice contributes to a larger narrative of self-determination.

The transition from survival to stewardship can be seen in practical examples where individuals transform small, routine financial decisions into expressions of vision and control. Take the case of Jamal, a gig worker whose income fluctuates unpredictably. For years, Jamal approached his finances with a survivalist urgency, allocating his earnings solely toward immediate bills. After engaging with a community finance programme focused on adaptive budgeting and goal-setting, he began to set aside small amounts regularly—even as little as £5 on days with surplus income. This modest act shifted his relationship with money; rather than seeing his finances as a source of anxiety, Jamal started to view them as a system he could influence. This emergent sense of stewardship motivated further engagement with saving and eventually small-scale investing. Jamal's story exemplifies how stewardship begins with reinterpreting financial decisions as meaningful commitments rather than unavoidable chores.

This reframing has profound psychological implications. Stewardship fosters *emotional return on investment*—a concept emphasised throughout this book—that centres agency, pride, and momentum before monetary growth. By consciously stewarding resources, individuals cultivate resilience against scarcity's psychological effects. The act of managing money with intention builds confidence and self-efficacy, which are essential precursors to sustained financial engagement. Unlike survival, which is reactive and often isolating, stewardship is proactive and generative, encouraging a sense of purpose and connectedness to one's financial future.

Importantly, stewardship acknowledges the complexity and messiness inherent in financial lives constrained by low or irregular incomes. It rejects the simplistic binary of success or failure embedded in many traditional financial narratives. Instead, it embraces *progressive realignment*—the idea that financial health is built through iterative adjustments, learning from setbacks, and celebrating small victories. This perspective counters the paralysis that scarcity often induces by validating incremental efforts and normalising fluctuation.

This shift also necessitates redefining what financial "success" looks like. Conventional metrics—such as net worth, investment returns, or savings targets—are often unrealistic benchmarks for those with limited means. Stewardship encourages alternative criteria rooted in *sustainability and alignment* with personal values and circumstances. It promotes cultivating a relationship with money characterised by mindfulness and intentionality rather than mere accumulation. Through this lens, wealth is less a static figure and more a dynamic practice of care and foresight.

Critically, the journey from survival to stewardship is not solely an individual endeavour but deeply shaped by context and community. Social support networks, culturally relevant financial education, and accessible financial tools play vital roles in facilitating this transition. Community-based initiatives that recognise and validate the experiences of low-income earners provide spaces where stewardship is modelled and reinforced. Peer learning and shared narratives help counter isolation and stigma, creating a collective momentum toward financial agency.

Technological innovations also contribute to enabling stewardship. Micro-investing platforms, automated savings apps, and budgeting tools designed for variable incomes lower barriers to participation. These tools operationalise stewardship by automating small, consistent financial acts, reducing cognitive load, and providing visual feedback that reinforces progress. However, technology is effective only when paired with mindset shifts and realistic expectations that acknowledge challenges rather than obscure them.

The conceptual tension between survival and stewardship reveals a broader ethical reflection on how societies value and support financial inclusion. Policies and systems that perpetuate economic precarity undermine opportunities for stewardship, entrenching cycles of scarcity and marginalisation. Recognising stewardship as a legitimate and vital form of financial practice demands not only individual empowerment but structural change. Access to affordable credit, living wages, and social safety nets are prerequisites that enable stewardship to flourish beyond mere aspiration.

Transitioning to stewardship involves cultivating *temporal perspective*—the ability to balance immediate needs with long-term goals. This temporal balancing act is particularly difficult under scarcity but is essential for breaking cycles of financial instability. Stewardship encourages developing rituals and habits that anchor financial behaviour in consistent, manageable actions aligned with one's vision. Whether it is setting aside a small weekly amount, reviewing expenses regularly, or engaging with financial learning, these practices gradually rewire the cognitive and emotional framework governing money management.

From a philosophical standpoint, stewardship aligns with concepts of *financial dignity* and *self-respect*. It positions money management not as a burden but as an expression of care for oneself and one's community. This reframing challenges narratives that equate low income with financial incompetence, offering instead a dignified approach that honours the realities and aspirations of all economic participants. It restores agency to those often written off by conventional finance, validating their capacity to steward resources with foresight and integrity.

Ultimately, the passage from survival to stewardship marks a critical inflection point in financial empowerment. It transforms financial decisions from reactive, anxiety-driven responses into purposeful, visionary acts that build momentum over time. This shift, grounded in emotional and behavioural insights, is both practical and profound. It equips readers to navigate economic constraints with renewed confidence, to claim their role as active architects of their financial futures, and to engage with investing not as an exclusive privilege but as a lived practice of stewardship and self-respect.

The Emotional ROI: A New Framework

Investing is typically framed as a matter of numbers, returns, and financial metrics—a discipline governed by percentages, compounding interest, and market performance. While these elements are undeniably important, this conventional framing neglects a crucial dimension: the emotional and psychological returns that investing generates long before any financial growth becomes visible. This oversight is particularly consequential for individuals starting with small or irregular incomes, for whom the monetary gains may seem distant or negligible. The concept of *Emotional Return on Investment* (Emotional ROI) offers a necessary recalibration. It foregrounds the agency, pride, and inner momentum cultivated through the act of investing itself, positioning these intangible rewards as foundational to building sustainable wealth. Introducing Emotional ROI reorients the conversation, setting a philosophical foundation that is as vital to the investor's journey as financial literacy or market strategy.

At its core, Emotional ROI recognises that investing is an expression of belief in one's future self—a practice of self-respect and empowerment. For many, the initial steps of investing, particularly when beginning with modest amounts, may not produce immediate financial gains. Yet these acts yield significant psychological dividends: the reclaiming of agency over one's financial narrative, the quiet pride of participation in an economic system often perceived as exclusionary, and the building of internal momentum that fosters continued engagement. Such emotional outcomes constitute a form of wealth in their own right—one that precedes and enables material accumulation.

Consider the case of Maria, a single mother working part-time, whose first investment was a £5 contribution to a micro-investing app. Financially, the return was negligible in the short term, but the emotional impact was profound. This initial act shifted her self-perception: she moved from seeing herself as a passive consumer trapped by circumstance to an active participant in shaping her financial future. This empowerment translated into greater financial discipline, curiosity, and confidence—qualities that catalysed subsequent savings and investments. Maria's experience exemplifies how Emotional ROI functions as a psychological lever, unlocking capacities essential for long-term wealth building.

The concept challenges traditional finance paradigms that prioritise external outcomes and often marginalise emotional and behavioural factors as secondary or irrelevant. These paradigms tend to privilege scale and immediacy of returns, which can alienate low-income earners for whom capital is scarce and the time horizon for growth is extended. Emotional ROI insists that the *process* of investing—marked by intentionality, consistency, and self-affirmation—is itself an investment with real, measurable value. This process builds the psychological infrastructure necessary for enduring financial success.

Psychologists have long understood the interplay between behaviour and identity. The theory of *self-efficacy*, pioneered by Albert Bandura, underscores how belief in one's capability to execute actions necessary to achieve goals is a critical determinant of behaviour and achievement. Emotional ROI embodies this principle within financial contexts, positing that the act of investing reinforces self-efficacy, which in turn sustains ongoing financial behaviours. Without this reinforcement, the challenges of economic precarity can erode motivation and lead to disengagement.

This insight has practical implications for how financial education and advice are structured. Emphasising Emotional ROI encourages a shift away from purely technical instruction toward holistic engagement that supports emotional and cognitive empowerment. It reframes small, consistent contributions as victories rather than trivialities, cultivating a positive feedback loop that nurtures financial identity. This reframing is essential for fostering resilience amid setbacks—market volatility, unexpected expenses, or missed contributions—and guards against the demoralisation that often accompanies early-stage investing.

Emotional ROI also intersects with behavioural economics, particularly the role of *mental accounting* and *loss aversion*. Investors frequently evaluate decisions based not solely on objective financial outcomes but on their emotional reactions to gains and losses. Recognising this, Emotional ROI integrates the understanding that positive emotional experiences—such as the pride from making an investment or the satisfaction of seeing a portfolio grow—are integral to sustaining investment behaviour. These experiences counterbalance the fear and uncertainty inherent in markets, especially for novices or those with limited financial cushions.

Furthermore, Emotional ROI connects to broader cultural and social dimensions of wealth-building. Historically, investing has been framed as an elite activity, often inaccessible or intimidating to low-income individuals. Engaging with investing through the lens of Emotional ROI challenges this exclusivity by validating the emotional and identity work that investing entails. It shifts the narrative from exclusion to inclusion, affirming that financial participation is not reserved for the affluent but is a universal avenue for expressing agency and hope.

This framework also invites ethical reflection on how society supports or hinders the cultivation of Emotional ROI. Financial institutions and educators frequently overlook the emotional labour involved in engaging with finance, particularly for marginalised populations. Designing tools, platforms, and educational programmes that acknowledge and foster Emotional ROI can democratise access and deepen engagement. For example, micro-investing apps that provide immediate, understandable feedback and celebrate milestones tap into this emotional dimension, making investing feel less abstract and more personally meaningful.

Critically, Emotional ROI does not diminish the importance of eventual financial returns; rather, it situates them within a broader matrix of outcomes where psychological and behavioural gains are prerequisites for material success. It acknowledges that financial growth is neither guaranteed nor immediate but can be facilitated by cultivating the internal conditions—agency, confidence, identity—that underpin sustained investing. This perspective reframes patience not as passive waiting but as active cultivation of the self as an investor.

From a philosophical standpoint, Emotional ROI aligns with notions of *wealth as a narrative*. Wealth is not merely a static sum but a story that individuals author about their relationship with money, their future, and themselves. Investing, understood emotionally, is a series of affirmations that rewrite limiting narratives of scarcity and helplessness. Each small investment is a chapter in this story, contributing to a cumulative transformation that transcends dollar amounts.

Ultimately, embracing Emotional ROI equips readers with a powerful conceptual tool that redefines success in investing. It validates the emotional labour inherent in beginning, persevering, and growing as an investor—especially for those starting with limited means. It reframes small contributions as meaningful acts of self-respect and agency, fostering momentum that is both internal and financial. This framework sets the philosophical and practical foundation for the entire book, anchoring the journey of building wealth not solely in markets but in the evolving identity of the investor.

Chapter 2
Building a Budget That Honors Reality (and Leaves Room for Growth)

Budgeting is too often reduced to a mechanical exercise—rows of numbers, rigid categories, and spreadsheets that attempt to impose order on financial chaos. Yet beneath this reductionist view lies a deeper truth: a budget is, in fact, a living narrative, a chronicle of one's values, priorities, and evolving identity. It tells the story of how we relate to money, the choices we make, and the vision we hold for our future. To craft a budget that truly serves—not merely as a ledger of constraints but as a scaffold for growth—requires recognising this narrative dimension. It calls for a shift from arithmetic to intentional authorship, where every financial decision reflects and shapes who we are becoming.

This chapter opens with a provocative framing: your budget is not just numbers on a spreadsheet but a biography of your financial self. Each expense, each allocation, forms a sentence in the story of your values and aspirations. Seen this way, budgeting becomes an act of self-expression rather than a chore. It exposes patterns of spending and saving that speak not only to external obligations but also to internal priorities. Investing in a course, a small indulgence, or a hobby conveys narratives about deservingness, potential, and foresight. Recognising this dimension allows readers to approach budgeting with curiosity and self-compassion, aligning present actions with longer-term ambitions.

Yet understanding the narrative nature of budgeting is only part of the solution. For many, it is entangled with a persistent psychological trap: the $0.00 shame loop. Shortfalls trigger shame, guilt, and avoidance, which in turn stall budgeting efforts and deepen distress. Negative balances, overdrafts, or missed allocations feed a spiral that erodes motivation and self-worth, extending beyond finances to affect mental health, relationships, and one's ability to engage constructively with money. This chapter explores the psychology behind this loop and offers practical strategies to interrupt it through adaptive, guilt-free budgeting systems. These systems prioritise flexibility and kindness, reframing "failures" as informative data rather than moral shortcomings, breaking cycles of shame, and enabling renewed progress.

Central to navigating this terrain is an appreciation of micro-margins—the seemingly trivial gaps in daily spending decisions. The common assumption that a few pounds here or there cannot make a difference is misleading. Harvesting these micro-margins, however, can transform financial outcomes over time. Think of it as "pocket composting": small scraps, individually inconsequential, collectively enrich the soil. Likewise, modest savings—skipping a daily coffee, adjusting utility usage, or capitalising on cashback offers—can accumulate into funds for investment or debt reduction. This chapter encourages mindfulness around these marginal decisions, recognising that wealth-building begins in subtle but potent shifts.

For many readers—freelancers, gig workers, or those with variable incomes—another critical dimension emerges: managing chaos and unpredictability. Traditional calendar-based budgets, designed for steady pay cycles, often fail in these contexts. Instead, this chapter introduces rhythm-based budgeting, a flexible, cyclical approach aligned with income patterns rather than fixed dates. Rhythm-based budgeting smooths volatility by identifying recurring income pulses and expense clusters, enabling buffers during high-income periods and scaled-back spending during lean phases. This approach reduces stress while fostering a proactive stance toward uncertainty.

Throughout the chapter, readers encounter both conceptual frameworks and concrete tools designed to construct budgets that honour reality while leaving room for growth. The emphasis is on cultivating a dynamic relationship with money—balancing discipline with compassion, foresight with flexibility. The aim is to move beyond zero-sum thinking, where budgets feel like cages, toward financial narratives that sustain momentum and open possibilities.

Integrating these insights, the chapter reframes budgeting as self-care and strategic visioning. Budgets are not merely restrictions but deliberate allocations toward what truly matters. By adopting guilt-free systems, harnessing micro-margins, and embracing rhythm over rigidity, readers can transform budgeting from anxiety-inducing obligation into a tool of empowerment. This transformation is foundational to investing with a small income and building enduring wealth.

Finally, the chapter honours the lived realities of those for whom budgeting is far from abstract. Financial lives are embedded in social, emotional, and practical contexts demanding nuanced approaches. The strategies offered respect these realities while expanding the horizon of possibility. Readers are invited not merely to manage scarcity but to author a budget biography that embodies resilience, intention, and growth—a story worth reading, revising, and celebrating as they move forward.

Your Budget is a Biography

Budgeting is often dismissed as a tedious, mechanical task—a series of calculations designed to corral spending into neat categories. This reduction strips budgeting of its deeper significance. Far from being merely a ledger of debits and credits, a budget is a rich, evolving narrative that reflects and shapes our values, identity, and aspirations. It is a biography written in financial terms, charting not only what we spend but who we are and who we intend to become. To treat a budget solely as a spreadsheet is to overlook its profound capacity to reveal the intimate relationship between money and selfhood.

Every financial choice embedded within a budget carries symbolic weight. When we allocate funds toward essentials such as housing or food, we are affirming priorities tied to safety and wellbeing. When we designate even modest sums for personal development, hobbies, or gifts, we articulate our values around growth, joy, and connection. These allocations are not arbitrary; they are chapters in a personal story of what matters most. Recognising this narrative dimension empowers individuals to approach budgeting with curiosity and intentionality, transforming it from a chore into a reflective practice that bridges present realities with future selves.

Consider the case of Alex, a graduate navigating entry-level employment with a modest income. Alex's budget initially reflected only survival needs—rent, transportation, food—without room for discretionary spending or savings. Over time, as financial literacy and self-awareness grew, Alex began reallocating small amounts toward courses, books, and social activities. These changes did more than adjust numbers; they signalled a shift in identity—from someone constrained by circumstance to an emerging investor in personal and financial growth. Alex's budget became a biography of transformation, each allocation narrating evolving values and aspirations.

This perspective challenges conventional budgeting advice that prioritises rigid categories and abstract optimisation over personal meaning. While traditional frameworks emphasise the "right" percentages to save or spend, they often fail to account for the emotional and identity work that budgets perform. By recasting budgets as autobiographical narratives, we invite a more holistic approach—one that honours complexity, contradiction, and the fluidity of human experience. Budgeting thus becomes a dynamic dialogue between current needs and future vision, a tool for self-discovery as much as financial management.

Mapping spending to identity also exposes cultural and psychological influences that shape financial behaviour. Money is rarely neutral; it is laden with inherited narratives about worth, success, and deservingness. For many, patterns of spending and saving echo familial legacies or societal expectations, some of which may reinforce scarcity or guilt. For instance, prioritising immediate consumption over saving might reflect an ingrained belief that "there will never be enough," while rigorous saving could be an expression of control in response to past instability. Recognising these underlying narratives enables readers to critically assess whether their budgets align with their authentic values or are constrained by unexamined conditioning.

Importantly, viewing budgets as biographies opens pathways for intentional revision and growth. Just as we rewrite personal stories through reflection and new experiences, so too can we revise our financial narratives. This process requires both honesty and compassion—acknowledging past patterns without judgement and embracing the possibility of change. Practical tools such as journaling about spending choices, setting values-based goals, or envisioning one's future self become integral to this narrative work. These practices deepen engagement with budgeting and foster alignment between financial behaviour and identity.

This conceptualisation also sheds light on the tensions that many experience between aspiration and reality. Budgets are not fixed scripts but living documents that must adapt to shifting circumstances, emotions, and goals. The biography metaphor captures this fluidity, reminding us that growth often entails messiness and recalibration. A budget that rigidly enforces deprivation may signal a punitive narrative of scarcity, whereas one that incorporates flexibility and celebration of small victories reflects a narrative of stewardship and resilience.

Moreover, this narrative approach has implications for how financial educators and advisors engage with clients. It calls for moving beyond prescriptive advice toward empathetic dialogue that honours the individual's story and context. By situating budgeting within identity formation, professionals can support clients in uncovering deeper motivations and barriers, thereby facilitating more sustainable financial behaviour. This shift from technique to narrative transforms budgeting from a compliance exercise into an empowering practice of self-authorship.

Emerging research in behavioural finance and psychology corroborates the importance of narrative in financial decision-making. Studies show that people are more motivated and consistent in their financial behaviours when these actions are connected to personally meaningful stories and identities. For example, framing saving as an investment in one's future self has been shown to increase saving rates and reduce impulsive spending. This evidence underscores that budgets are not merely functional tools but psychological landscapes where identity and behaviour intersect.

Finally, recognising a budget as a biography invites readers to reclaim agency over their financial stories. It challenges fatalistic views that external circumstances wholly determine financial outcomes and instead highlights the active role individuals play in shaping their economic lives through meaning-making and intentional choice.

This empowerment is particularly vital for those starting with small or variable incomes, who may feel excluded from conventional narratives of financial success. By embracing budgeting as narrative, they can author stories of resilience, growth, and possibility, regardless of current limitations.

In reframing budgets as biographies, this chapter offers a foundational lens through which readers can engage more deeply with their finances. It transforms budgeting from a task of restriction to a practice of self-expression and future-building. By mapping spending to identity and future self, individuals gain not only clearer financial direction but also richer insight into who they are and who they aspire to be. This narrative approach lays the groundwork for the adaptive, compassionate, and growth-oriented budgeting systems explored throughout this chapter and the broader book.

The $0.00 Shame Loop

The moment a bank balance hits zero—or worse, dips into the red—a potent and often invisible psychological reaction takes hold. This reaction, which can be termed the *$0.00 shame loop*, is more than a fleeting feeling of discomfort; it is a deep, self-reinforcing spiral of shame, anxiety, and avoidance that undermines both financial stability and emotional wellbeing. The loop begins when negative balances trigger internalised narratives of failure and inadequacy, which then erode motivation and foster behaviours that perpetuate financial distress. Understanding this loop is crucial for anyone seeking to break free from cycles of scarcity and build sustainable budgeting practices. More importantly, recognising the psychological dynamics at play allows for the design of adaptive, guilt-free budgeting systems that prevent shame spirals and foster resilience.

At first glance, a negative bank balance might appear as a simple technical problem—a shortage of funds to cover expenditures. However, its psychological impact is profound and multifaceted. The $0.00 shame loop arises from the intersection of economic reality and self-perception, where the experience of insufficient funds is internalised as a personal shortcoming. Studies in behavioural psychology reveal that shame is a powerful emotion linked to feelings of worthlessness and social rejection. Unlike guilt, which relates to specific actions, shame attacks the core self, leading to avoidance behaviours such as evading financial tasks, ignoring bills, or disengaging from budgeting altogether. These avoidance strategies, though understandable, exacerbate financial instability, creating a vicious cycle that deepens both fiscal and emotional deficits.

The social context further compounds this dynamic. Financial hardship is often stigmatised, reinforcing isolation and self-blame. Cultural narratives valorise financial competence and success, implicitly casting those struggling with money as failures. This societal lens magnifies the internal shame triggered by a $0.00 balance, transforming it from a numerical state into a marker of identity. The psychological burden is not merely about money but about perceived self-worth and social belonging. The resultant shame loop is therefore not just a cognitive distortion but a lived experience with tangible consequences on mental health and behaviour.

Empirical research supports the existence and impact of such shame-driven financial behaviours. For example, a 2019 study published in the *Journal of Consumer Research* found that individuals experiencing financial shame were more likely to delay bill payments, avoid bank communications, and underutilise financial support resources. These avoidance behaviours create feedback loops that worsen financial standing, reinforcing shame and hopelessness. The challenge is that traditional budgeting advice—often framed in terms of discipline and responsibility—can inadvertently intensify this shame, further alienating individuals caught in the loop.

Breaking the $0.00 shame loop requires more than exhortations to "budget better" or "spend less." It demands a fundamental shift in how budgeting systems are designed and experienced, particularly for those with limited or variable incomes. Adaptive budgeting systems prioritise *guilt-free flexibility* and acknowledge the inevitability of setbacks and volatility. These systems replace rigid prescriptions with responsive frameworks that accommodate fluctuations, celebrate incremental progress, and view "failures" as opportunities for learning rather than moral lapses.

One practical approach is the implementation of *buffer zones* within budgeting. Instead of aiming for a zero balance at the end of each budgeting period, adaptive systems encourage maintaining small positive buffers—however modest—that cushion against unexpected expenses or income delays. This strategy helps prevent the triggering event of a zero or negative balance, thereby interrupting the shame cycle before it escalates. Although seemingly small, these buffers carry outsized psychological benefits, providing a sense of control and security that fosters proactive financial behaviour.

Another critical element is reframing budgeting language and goals to remove moral judgement. Instead of metrics centred on "perfect adherence" or "zero deviation," adaptive systems adopt language that normalises fluctuation and emphasises *progress over perfection.* This shift encourages users to track and reflect on patterns without self-criticism, thereby reducing the emotional weight associated with budgeting challenges. For instance, journals or apps that prompt users to note "lessons learned" rather than "failures" cultivate a growth mindset that sustains engagement even during difficult periods.

Technology also offers promising tools to counteract shame spirals. Automated savings features, micro-investing platforms, and real-time spending alerts can reduce cognitive load and increase financial visibility without overwhelming users. Importantly, these tools succeed when designed with empathy—offering encouragement, celebrating small wins, and avoiding punitive notifications that may trigger shame. User interfaces that prioritise kindness and clarity over complexity can transform budgeting from a source of stress into a source of empowerment.

Case studies illuminate how these principles operate in real life. Take Emma, a freelance graphic designer with inconsistent monthly income who frequently faced zero or negative balances. Traditional budgeting models left her discouraged and disengaged. After adopting an adaptive budgeting approach that incorporated buffer zones and flexible spending categories, Emma reported reduced anxiety and greater confidence. The system allowed her to "pause" certain discretionary expenses during lean months without guilt, enabling her to maintain basic financial stability and gradually build savings. This practical flexibility disrupted her previous shame spiral and fostered a more sustainable financial rhythm.

The $0.00 shame loop also invites critical ethical reflection on broader systemic factors. Financial systems often penalise those with precarious incomes through overdraft fees, punitive credit scoring, and limited access to affordable credit, effectively institutionalising shame. Recognising this structural dimension shifts responsibility beyond individual behaviour to include advocacy for more equitable financial products and policies. In this context, adaptive budgeting is not a substitute for systemic reform but a vital strategy that empowers individuals within imperfect systems.

From a psychological standpoint, combating shame loops aligns with principles of *self-compassion* and *emotional regulation*. Research in clinical psychology indicates that cultivating self-compassion reduces shame's intensity and fosters adaptive coping strategies. Budgeting systems and financial education programmes that integrate these principles—encouraging users to treat themselves with kindness and recognise common humanity in financial struggles—can break the isolation that shame engenders. This integration transforms budgeting from a punitive task into a supportive practice of resilience building.

Importantly, preventing shame spirals does not entail lowering standards or abdicating responsibility but reframing responsibility in a manner that honours complexity and imperfection. It recognises that financial lives, especially those on modest incomes, are fraught with uncertainty and emotional challenge. Adaptive, guilt-free budgeting systems empower individuals to navigate this terrain with grace, maintaining motivation and engagement over the long term.

Understanding and addressing the $0.00 shame loop is therefore foundational to building financial resilience. It reveals how psychological barriers can entrench economic hardship and how thoughtful system design can foster sustainable change. By moving beyond shame-based models and embracing adaptive, compassionate budgeting, individuals reclaim agency over their finances and break free from cycles of scarcity and self-judgment.

This shift is not merely technical but transformative, laying essential groundwork for the consistent, confident investment practices that follow in this book.

Micro-Margins that Matter

In the landscape of personal finance, grand gestures and substantial windfalls often capture the imagination. Yet, the transformative power of *micro-margins*—those seemingly insignificant amounts like £3 saved here or £7 trimmed there—is frequently overlooked or dismissed. This oversight is a critical blind spot, especially for individuals with modest or variable incomes, where the accumulation of small gaps can be the linchpin for financial stability and growth. Understanding how to deliberately identify, cultivate, and harvest these micro-margins redefines wealth-building not as a distant ambition but as a practical, accessible process grounded in everyday choices. The metaphor of micro-margins as the "compost of finance" offers a vivid lens: just as tiny scraps of organic matter break down to nourish fertile soil, small financial adjustments collectively enrich one's economic ecosystem over time.

The first insight to grasp is that micro-margins are not accidental leftovers but *intentional spaces* within a budget or spending pattern that can be cultivated. They arise from minute decisions—skipping an impulsive purchase, switching to a less expensive service, or claiming a small cashback reward. Individually, these savings may seem trivial, even negligible. However, when systematically identified and redirected toward financial goals—whether debt repayment, emergency funds, or investment—their cumulative effect can be substantial. Behavioural finance research supports this, highlighting the power of incremental changes that are psychologically sustainable and more resistant to burnout than radical overhauls.

Consider the example of Jasmine, a part-time retail worker who struggled with variable income and limited discretionary funds. By tracking daily spending with a focus on micro-margins—such as foregoing a £2.50 snack, adjusting energy consumption to save £4 weekly, and utilising a £1 cashback app—Jasmine created a modest but consistent savings stream. Over 18 months, these small gains amounted to over £500, which she invested in a low-cost index fund.

Jasmine's case illustrates that micro-margins are not about deprivation but *strategic moderation* and conscious prioritisation. They enable participation in wealth-building activities without drastic lifestyle sacrifices, fostering both financial and emotional sustainability.

The deliberate harvesting of micro-margins challenges common assumptions embedded in mainstream finance, which often emphasise large-scale budgeting and high minimum savings rates. Such approaches can feel inaccessible or discouraging to many, reinforcing the myth that meaningful financial progress requires large, immediate surpluses. Micro-margins dismantle this myth by legitimising small-scale action as both valid and effective. This perspective aligns with emerging financial technologies—such as round-up savings apps and fractional investing platforms—that operationalise micro-margins by automating the capture of small amounts, thereby reducing cognitive load and psychological resistance.

The metaphor of micro-margins as compost extends beyond financial mechanics to embody a mindset of *patience and nourishment.* Composting is a slow, natural process where organic fragments break down to feed new growth. Similarly, micro-margins accumulate gradually, nourishing the soil of one's financial health and enabling richer, more sustainable wealth cultivation. This analogy emphasises that wealth-building is not solely about immediate returns but about creating fertile conditions for future growth. It invites readers to reconceive small financial actions as investments in the *environment* of their economic lives, laying groundwork that supports resilience and opportunity.

Yet, harvesting micro-margins requires discipline and intentionality often absent in day-to-day financial routines. This is where habit formation intersects with micro-margins. Research from behavioural psychology underscores that small, repeated behaviours anchored to existing routines are more likely to persist and compound. For example, linking the decision to save small amounts with routine activities—such as setting aside £5 on payday or reallocating money saved from cancelled subscriptions—turns micro-margins into sustainable habits. Over time, these habits create a positive feedback loop, reinforcing self-efficacy and financial identity.

The ethical dimensions of micro-margins merit reflection. Encouraging small savings or investments can empower individuals often excluded from conventional financial systems, promoting inclusivity and equity. However, there is a risk of *micro-exploitation* if financial products disproportionately extract value through fees or obscure costs at the micro-level. Critical awareness and consumer education are essential to ensure that the harvesting of micro-margins benefits individuals rather than financial intermediaries. Transparency and regulation play pivotal roles in safeguarding the interests of those who rely on these small-scale financial mechanisms.

Contrasting perspectives on micro-margins also illuminate conceptual tensions. Critics might argue that focusing on tiny savings detracts attention from systemic issues such as wage stagnation, housing unaffordability, or credit access. While these structural challenges undoubtedly shape financial realities, embracing micro-margins does not negate the need for systemic reform; rather, it equips individuals with tools to navigate and optimise within current constraints. Micro-margins serve as *both a practical strategy and a psychological anchor*—providing immediate agency while supporting broader aspirations.

Moreover, micro-margins highlight the interplay between *quantitative* and *qualitative* dimensions of wealth. Financial calculations alone do not capture the emotional significance of micro-margins as symbols of control, progress, and hope. For example, consciously redirecting £3 saved from a habitual expense toward a meaningful goal can bolster motivation and reinforce a positive financial narrative. This qualitative dimension strengthens commitment and resilience, bridging the gap between abstract financial planning and lived experience.

In sum, micro-margins transform the concept of financial capability from an exclusive pursuit requiring abundant resources into an inclusive, actionable framework grounded in everyday realities. They invite a paradigm shift that values *consistency over scale* and *intentionality over perfection.* By attending to the smallest gaps and choices, readers can cultivate a sustainable foundation for wealth accumulation—one that honours their present context while expanding their future possibilities.

Harnessing micro-margins requires not only awareness but deliberate cultivation through adaptive strategies, habit integration, and critical engagement with financial products and systems. This approach reframes wealth-building as a gradual, organic process akin to nurturing a garden—where small seeds, carefully planted and tended, eventually yield abundant harvests. Embracing this perspective empowers readers to reclaim agency over their finances, transforming micro-margins from overlooked fragments into the fertile ground from which lasting financial wellbeing grows.

Budgeting When Life is Chaotic

For freelancers, gig workers, and those earning irregular incomes, budgeting often feels like trying to map a shifting coastline with a straightedge. Traditional budgeting models, designed around predictable monthly paychecks and fixed billing cycles, fall short in capturing the volatility and uncertainty inherent to these financial realities. This mismatch breeds frustration and disengagement, as rigid frameworks fail to accommodate the ebb and flow of inconsistent earnings. To build financial stability amid such chaos requires more than standard tools—it demands a paradigm shift toward rhythm-based budgeting, an adaptive approach that aligns financial planning with the natural cadences of variable income. This chapter introduces practical strategies that honour the unpredictability of chaotic earnings while fostering agency and growth.

At its core, rhythm-based budgeting rejects the assumption that income and expenses neatly conform to calendar months. Instead, it acknowledges that earnings may arrive sporadically—lumpsums at irregular intervals, payments contingent on project completion, or fluctuating hours that defy standard pay cycles. Attempting to impose a date-based budget onto this fluid context often results in cognitive dissonance and emotional distress. For instance, a freelancer might receive a substantial payment one month and minimal or no income the next, yet face monthly expenses like rent that demand consistent payment. Traditional budgets, which allocate fixed amounts monthly, can amplify stress by obscuring how to balance immediate obligations with uneven cash flow.

Rhythm-based budgeting responds to this challenge by framing financial planning around income *cycles* or *rhythms* rather than fixed dates. Rather than organising budgets by calendar month, individuals map income as it arrives and distribute expenses over these income cycles, which may span varying lengths depending on earning patterns. This fluid framework allows for the creation of flexible spending and saving plans that smooth out volatility. For example, a gig worker who receives payments biweekly or irregularly might budget based on each payment cycle, ensuring that essential expenses are covered immediately while allocating residual funds toward savings or discretionary spending. By synchronising budgets with income rhythms, individuals regain control and reduce the cognitive burden of unpredictable finances.

Practical implementation of rhythm-based budgeting begins with *tracking income patterns* over several months to identify natural cycles. This involves recording payment dates, amounts, and frequency, then segmenting budgets accordingly. Such tracking may reveal, for instance, that income spikes monthly with certain clients or fluctuates seasonally. Armed with this data, individuals can allocate funds to cover fixed expenses in advance and earmark surplus funds for leaner periods. This anticipatory budgeting transforms financial chaos into manageable patterns, enabling proactive rather than reactive decision-making.

An illustrative case is that of Daniel, a freelance writer whose income varied dramatically month to month. Traditional monthly budgeting left him anxious and frequently short on funds. After adopting rhythm-based budgeting, Daniel segmented his income into "cycles" aligned with invoice payments, allowing him to prioritise bills and set aside emergency funds during high-earning periods. This approach eased his financial stress and provided a clearer picture of available resources, facilitating incremental investments and debt reduction. Daniel's experience underscores the empowerment rhythm-based budgeting offers by aligning financial planning with lived income realities.

Rhythm-based budgeting also demands adaptive strategies for variable expenses. Rather than assuming static monthly bills, individuals categorise expenses as fixed, variable, or periodic and adjust allocations based on income within each cycle. This flexible categorisation allows for scaling discretionary spending without compromising essentials. For example, a gig worker might reduce non-essential spending during lean cycles but maintain payments toward debts or savings. This nuanced flexibility respects both financial constraints and personal wellbeing, fostering sustainable budgeting habits.

Critically, rhythm-based budgeting intersects with behavioural economics insights about mental accounting and loss aversion. When budgeting is rigid and fails to reflect income variability, individuals experience heightened anxiety and are prone to "all-or-nothing" financial decisions, such as abandoning budgets after minor setbacks. Rhythm-based models, by contrast, promote incremental adjustments and tolerate fluctuation, reducing the emotional volatility associated with budgeting. This emotional regulation is vital for sustaining engagement and preventing burnout, especially for those juggling multiple income streams.

The shift toward rhythm-based budgeting also raises important considerations about systemic and structural factors influencing income instability. While adaptive budgeting equips individuals with tools to manage variability, it does not negate the challenges posed by precarious labour markets, lack of social safety nets, or income insecurity. Recognising these broader contexts is essential for a holistic understanding of financial stability. Adaptive budgeting strategies must therefore be complemented by advocacy for policy reforms that enhance income security and worker protections, creating an environment where rhythm-based budgeting can be most effective.

Technology plays a significant role in operationalising rhythm-based budgeting. Emerging financial apps and platforms now offer features tailored to irregular income earners, such as real-time income tracking, flexible categorisation of expenses, and automated savings triggered by payment cycles. These tools reduce the cognitive demands of manual budgeting and provide timely feedback that reinforces financial discipline. However, technology must be accessible, user-friendly, and designed with empathy to truly support those navigating chaotic incomes. Otherwise, digital complexity risks replicating exclusionary patterns found in traditional finance.

From a philosophical perspective, rhythm-based budgeting invites a redefinition of financial "normalcy." It challenges the implicit bias that steady, predictable paychecks are the standard and instead validates diverse economic experiences. This inclusive stance recognises that financial planning is not one-size-fits-all but must be tailored to the rhythms of individual lives. Such recognition fosters dignity and agency, countering narratives that marginalise irregular earners as financially irresponsible or unstable.

Furthermore, rhythm-based budgeting promotes a mindset of *financial stewardship* over scarcity-driven survival. By aligning planning with income flows and building buffers during prosperous cycles, individuals cultivate resilience and a proactive relationship with money. This approach encourages viewing budgeting not as a restrictive chore but as a dynamic, creative process of shaping one's economic future despite unpredictability.

In practice, embracing rhythm-based budgeting requires iterative learning and patience. It demands attention to patterns, willingness to adjust plans, and acceptance of imperfect consistency. These qualities—flexibility, awareness, and self-compassion—are often undervalued in financial discourse but are essential for those whose economic lives defy linear models. Support networks, peer learning, and accessible education can bolster this adaptive capacity, providing both technical skills and emotional encouragement.

In summary, budgeting when life is chaotic calls for frameworks and tools that honour income variability and personal realities. Rhythm-based budgeting offers a viable, empowering alternative to date-based models, transforming financial unpredictability into navigable patterns. It fosters agency, reduces anxiety, and lays groundwork for incremental growth. For freelancers, gig workers, and variable earners, mastering rhythm-based budgeting is not merely a financial strategy—it is an essential act of reclaiming control and cultivating a sustainable, hopeful economic identity.

Chapter 3
Saving Is Investing's First Muscle

Saving rarely receives the attention it deserves in discussions of wealth building. It is the quiet, unsung act that precedes the more celebrated milestones of investing and portfolio growth. To bypass saving is akin to attempting a strenuous workout without first stretching—skipping the preparation that makes performance sustainable. This chapter frames saving not as a dull prerequisite, but as the foundational discipline, the psychological warm-up essential for long-term financial success. Drawing on analogies from athletics, habit formation, and craftsmanship, it demonstrates how the rigour of saving cultivates a mindset in which discipline matures into opportunity, setting the stage for more ambitious financial ventures.

The fitness analogy proves instructive. Just as athletes build strength and endurance before mastering complex techniques, investors must develop the muscle of saving before navigating the subtleties of markets and asset allocation. Saving nurtures patience, self-control, and foresight—qualities indispensable to investing yet cultivated long before capital is deployed. This process demands confronting discomfort, resisting immediate gratification, and persisting without external validation. Paradoxically, it is precisely in this "mundane" repetition that the foundation for financial resilience and autonomy is laid.

Attention is given to the unique challenges faced by non-traditional earners: freelancers, gig workers, and those with fluctuating incomes. Conventional guidance—such as maintaining three to six months of expenses or automating transfers on payday—often fails in these contexts. Instead, the chapter proposes adaptable strategies aligned with variable income realities. Tiered savings models, beginning with modest targets like £50 and advancing through £200 and £800 milestones, enable readers to calibrate ambition to circumstance. This flexible scaffolding accommodates financial volatility while fostering incremental progress.

Central to these strategies is the behavioural insight known as the "Invisible Account" trick—a practical, psychologically informed method for shielding savings from impulsive withdrawals. By automating transfers into accounts or digital tools that are deliberately out of immediate reach, savers sidestep temptation. This subtle tactic introduces an element of play and agency into what might otherwise feel rigid or joyless, transforming saving into a dynamic, interactive practice. The chapter unpacks how leveraging inertia and reducing cognitive friction makes consistent saving more achievable and sustainable.

Equally significant is the chapter's challenge to prevailing narratives that stigmatise modest or irregular saving. Many low-income earners experience shame or discouragement when their savings fall short of idealised benchmarks. Such emotional burdens erode motivation. By normalising all forms of saving—including irregular, small, or "imperfect" contributions—the chapter reframes these acts as meaningful victories rather than failures. It provides conceptual language and frameworks to celebrate incremental progress, fostering self-compassion and long-term commitment.

Weaving these themes together, the chapter repositions saving from a peripheral, tedious task to the first essential muscle flexed in wealth creation. It invites readers to approach saving as an adaptive, identity-shaping practice—one that conditions behaviour and mindset for the more complex demands of investing. By integrating psychological insight, practical adaptation, and compassionate reframing, the chapter presents a roadmap for cultivating financial discipline amid uncertainty and scarcity.

Readers are guided not only toward strategies that fit their financial realities but also toward a mindset that honours small, incremental wins. This perspective challenges orthodoxies in finance and promotes an inclusive, sustainable vision of wealth-building—one in which saving is celebrated as the indispensable first step, the foundational muscle that enables all subsequent growth.

Why You Can't Skip the Boring Part

Saving money is often dismissed as dull, an unremarkable task overshadowed by the allure of investing and wealth accumulation.

Yet, this "boring" step is not a mere prelude or inconvenience; it is the essential psychological warm-up that conditions the mind, habits, and discipline necessary for successful investing. Skipping saving is akin to an athlete neglecting foundational training and leaping directly into competition—it undermines performance and sustainability. This chapter explores why saving, though unsexy, is the crucible in which financial resilience and identity are forged, using rich analogies from fitness, habit-building, and craft to demonstrate how discipline, developed through saving, ultimately shapes destiny.

The analogy with fitness is compelling. Physical training is a process grounded in repetition, incremental improvement, and the mastery of fundamentals before pursuing specialised skills or peak performance. Runners build endurance through steady mileage; weightlifters develop muscle through consistent, often unglamorous sets. Similarly, saving cultivates *financial endurance*—the capacity to delay gratification, manage uncertainty, and maintain consistent effort despite external distractions or internal resistance. Just as skipping warm-ups increases injury risk and reduces performance, neglecting saving undermines one's ability to engage confidently and sustainably with investing. The act of saving exercises discipline muscles that remain dormant without regular, conscious effort.

The science of habit formation offers further illumination. Saving is not only about accumulating funds but about embedding behaviours that reinforce self-efficacy and financial identity. Behavioural psychologist BJ Fogg emphasises that habits form through small, repeatable actions anchored to existing routines. Saving regularly, even in modest amounts, creates a feedback loop where success builds motivation and self-trust. This iterative process transforms saving from a task into a defining behaviour—a financial habit that supports more complex and higher-stakes activities like investing. Without this foundational habit, investing risks becoming sporadic, impulsive, or emotionally fraught.

Craftsmanship, too, provides a valuable parallel. Craftspeople understand that mastery arises from sustained attention to detail, practice, and patience. The "boring" work—repetitive sanding, meticulous stitching, careful calibration—builds the skills and discipline that allow for creativity and excellence later. Saving mirrors this dynamic: it requires steady, sometimes tedious effort, yet it is within this effort that the architecture of financial mastery is constructed. The process demands humility and patience, qualities often sidelined in narratives that glorify rapid wealth accumulation or market timing.

A case study from behavioural finance highlights the risks of bypassing saving's foundational role. Individuals who enter investing without an established savings buffer frequently exhibit heightened emotional volatility, reacting impulsively to market fluctuations or unexpected expenses. This emotional instability can lead to poor investment decisions, such as panic selling or excessive risk-taking, undermining long-term outcomes. Conversely, those with a solid savings "muscle" demonstrate greater psychological resilience, enabling disciplined investing and strategic risk management. This evidence underscores that saving cultivates not only financial capital but crucial emotional and cognitive resources.

The chapter also addresses common misconceptions that paint saving as an obstacle or delay to investing. Such views often emerge from cultural narratives valuing quick gains and undervaluing slow, steady progress. By reframing saving as the active, strategic development of financial capacity, the chapter challenges these misconceptions and elevates saving to a status commensurate with its foundational role. This reframing empowers readers to embrace saving as a meaningful practice integral to their investor identity rather than a frustrating barrier.

Importantly, the discipline cultivated through saving extends beyond financial realms into broader aspects of life. Research in psychology shows that self-regulation in one domain often transfers to others, fostering overall wellbeing and goal attainment. Thus, the commitment to saving not only prepares individuals for investing but also strengthens general capacities for planning, delay of gratification, and resilience. This interconnection highlights saving as a holistic practice of self-care and future orientation.

Furthermore, the chapter recognises that saving is often undervalued because it lacks immediate, tangible rewards. Unlike the thrill of investing gains or the satisfaction of large purchases, saving's benefits are latent, accruing over time. This temporal delay requires cultivating patience and trust—qualities fostered through experience and reinforced by consistent practice. The chapter offers strategies for maintaining motivation during this "boring" phase, including goal-setting, visualisation, and reframing savings as investments in identity and agency.

The psychological importance of discipline as destiny is also unpacked. Discipline is not mere self-control but an adaptive capacity shaped by environment, mindset, and experience. The process of saving systematically builds this capacity, transforming financial behaviours from reactive responses to intentional, values-aligned actions. Over time, disciplined saving crystallises into a durable identity—a "saver" who is equipped to engage with investing thoughtfully and confidently.

Balancing this emphasis on discipline, the chapter avoids valorising austerity or perfectionism. It acknowledges the realities of scarcity and fluctuating income, encouraging readers to approach saving with flexibility and self-compassion. Discipline, in this context, is framed as persistence rather than rigidity—a continuous commitment to progress rather than flawless execution. This nuanced perspective supports sustainable behaviour change and counters discouragement common among those facing financial instability.

Finally, the chapter situates saving within a broader social and cultural context. It critiques dominant financial narratives that glamorise risk and reward while marginalising the unglamorous but essential work of building financial foundations. By reclaiming the value of saving as the psychological warm-up for investing, the chapter contributes to a more inclusive and realistic discourse on wealth-building—one that honours process, patience, and personal growth alongside outcomes.

Engaging with saving as the foundational muscle for investing transforms it from a tedious necessity into a powerful practice of preparation and empowerment. This chapter invites readers to embrace the "boring part" not as a detour but as the deliberate training ground where financial discipline, identity, and resilience are forged—preparing them not only to invest but to thrive over the long term.

Emergency Funds for the Non-Traditional Earner

The concept of an emergency fund is a cornerstone of personal finance wisdom—a financial buffer intended to absorb shocks and provide security in the face of unexpected expenses or income disruptions. Yet the standard advice to accumulate three to six months' worth of expenses often assumes a steady, predictable income stream and a stable expense pattern. For non-traditional earners—freelancers, gig workers, part-time contractors, and others navigating fluctuating or uncertain income—this model is not only impractical but can feel demoralising. Conventional benchmarks fail to account for the irregular rhythms and unique vulnerabilities of variable earners, necessitating adapted strategies that both reflect and respect their realities. This chapter unpacks the complexities of emergency savings for non-traditional income streams and introduces tiered, flexible savings models designed to align with diverse financial circumstances, ultimately fostering resilience without overwhelming pressure.

At first glance, the challenges non-traditional earners face in building emergency funds are intuitive. Unlike salaried workers with predictable pay cycles, freelancers and gig workers may experience periods of feast and famine, with income varying dramatically month to month. Expenses may also shift in response to workload or seasonality, complicating the identification of a stable "baseline" for savings targets. Moreover, the absence of employer-provided benefits such as paid leave or unemployment insurance intensifies the stakes of financial precarity. The precariousness of income thus renders traditional savings goals not only daunting but often unattainable, undermining motivation and perpetuating financial insecurity.

Adapting emergency fund strategies to this context requires nuanced understanding and practical flexibility. Tiered savings models offer a framework for progressive resilience, encouraging readers to establish achievable, incremental goals that build toward comprehensive security over time. Instead of an immediate six-month reserve, tiered models might begin with a modest £50 emergency buffer, advancing to £200 and ultimately to a target of £800 or more, calibrated to individual circumstances. This approach recognises that *financial resilience is not binary but gradational*, and that initial savings—even if small—carry outsized psychological and practical value. Early victories bolster confidence and reduce the paralyzing effect of overwhelming targets, fostering momentum for sustained saving.

The tiered approach also facilitates adaptability. Non-traditional earners can adjust their savings pace in response to income fluctuations, contributing more during prosperous periods and pausing during leaner times without abandoning their goals entirely. This flexibility mitigates guilt and discouragement, key emotional barriers that traditional "all or nothing" savings advice often overlooks. Moreover, breaking emergency funds into tiers allows for prioritisation of liquidity and accessibility—early tiers may be held in immediately available accounts for urgent use, while later tiers might be directed toward slightly less liquid vehicles that offer higher returns, balancing readiness with growth potential.

Real-world examples illustrate the efficacy of tiered emergency funds. Take Lisa, a part-time illustrator whose monthly income swings unpredictably. By committing to a £50 starter fund, she built a psychological safety net that reduced anxiety and empowered better financial decision-making. Progressing to higher tiers over eighteen months, Lisa enhanced her capacity to absorb unexpected expenses such as equipment repair or medical bills without resorting to high-interest credit. Her experience highlights how tiered models transform emergency savings from abstract ideals into tangible, manageable steps tailored to volatile incomes.

In operationalising tiered savings, behavioural insights prove indispensable. Automating transfers—even modest amounts—into designated emergency accounts leverages inertia and minimises reliance on fluctuating motivation. Using separate accounts or sub-accounts earmarked for different tiers creates clear mental boundaries, reducing the temptation to raid emergency funds for discretionary spending. These mechanisms embed discipline while preserving flexibility, crucial for sustaining savings habits amid income instability.

The chapter also engages with broader conceptual tensions around financial security and precarity. While emergency funds enhance individual resilience, they coexist with systemic issues such as wage volatility, inadequate social protections, and precarious labour markets that constrain financial stability. Recognising this interplay underscores that emergency savings are a *necessary but insufficient* response to economic uncertainty. Advocacy for structural reform complements individual strategies, pointing toward a comprehensive approach to financial wellbeing.

Ethical considerations emerge in evaluating the burden emergency savings place on non-traditional earners. The expectation that individuals alone bear responsibility for buffering against systemic instability risks exacerbating inequality and obscuring social responsibility. This awareness informs the chapter's compassionate tone, which emphasises realistic goal-setting and self-compassion over unrealistic perfection. It calls for societal recognition of the unique challenges faced by variable earners and the creation of supportive frameworks that enhance, rather than solely rely on, personal savings.

Financial education tailored to non-traditional earners plays a vital role in translating tiered emergency fund concepts into practice. Educational interventions that incorporate relatable scenarios, culturally relevant narratives, and actionable steps improve comprehension and engagement. Peer support networks and community-based programmes further reinforce saving behaviours by normalising challenges and sharing practical solutions, fostering social capital that complements individual efforts.

Technological advancements enhance the feasibility of tiered emergency savings. Financial apps increasingly offer features such as customizable savings goals, automated contributions aligned with income patterns, and real-time tracking that accommodates irregular inflows. These tools reduce cognitive load and provide motivational feedback, essential for maintaining commitment. However, accessibility remains a concern; technology must be designed with inclusivity, affordability, and user experience in mind to truly benefit those with fluctuating incomes.

Philosophically, tiered emergency funds invite a reframing of financial preparedness as an evolving practice rather than a fixed milestone. This dynamic perspective honours the fluidity of non-traditional incomes and the adaptability required to navigate economic uncertainty. It positions saving as a form of *financial stewardship*—an ongoing commitment to care for one's present needs and future possibilities within complex realities.

In synthesising these insights, the chapter equips readers to approach emergency funds not as rigid targets but as flexible frameworks that align with their unique financial rhythms. It offers a pathway that balances pragmatism with aspiration, recognising that resilience is built through cumulative, manageable steps. By embracing tiered savings models, non-traditional earners can cultivate financial buffers that provide security and psychological relief, laying a foundation for more confident engagement with investing and long-term wealth-building.

This approach transforms emergency savings from an abstract ideal into an actionable, compassionate strategy that honours the lived experience of variable earners. It restores agency and hope where traditional advice falls short, affirming that financial stability is attainable through adaptive, intentional practice—even amid uncertainty.

The "Invisible Account" Trick

Saving money can often feel like a constant battle against one's own impulses, especially when every penny counts and the temptation to spend looms large. For many, the struggle isn't just about having enough but about managing the psychological friction that arises when savings are too visible, too accessible, or too easy to dip into. The "Invisible Account" trick emerges as a behavioural hack that cleverly sidesteps this challenge: by hiding savings from oneself using automation and app features, it transforms saving from a rigid chore into a game of stealth and surprise. This approach harnesses human psychology—specifically, the power of out-of-sight-out-of-mind—to foster consistent saving habits while reducing temptation and decision fatigue. Understanding and applying this trick injects a fresh sense of playfulness and strategy into what might otherwise feel like an onerous financial task.

At the heart of the Invisible Account concept is the recognition that *visibility breeds vulnerability*. When savings are too transparent—held in the same account as spending money or easily accessible via multiple taps—they become targets for spontaneous withdrawal. This accessibility, while convenient, undermines the discipline necessary to build meaningful reserves, especially for those with limited income or unpredictable expenses. Behavioural economics research highlights how immediate gratification often trumps long-term goals, particularly when the rewards of saving are abstract or deferred. The more salient and tangible the saved funds are, the greater the temptation to reallocate them toward pressing or impulsive expenditures.

Automation provides a practical solution by creating a form of financial *invisibility*. Automated transfers move money seamlessly and regularly into separate accounts or sub-accounts designed to be less accessible or visible. This process reduces cognitive load—eliminating the need for daily saving decisions—and leverages inertia, making saving the default rather than a negotiation. The Invisible Account, therefore, is less about secrecy and more about *strategic disconnection*—removing the saved funds from everyday consciousness to preserve them for their intended purpose.

Technological innovations have accelerated the feasibility of this behavioural hack. Modern banking apps and fintech platforms increasingly offer features that enable users to create multiple "pockets" or "vaults" within their primary accounts. These sub-accounts can be named, locked, or hidden from main dashboards, providing both psychological and functional barriers to impulsive access. For example, apps like Monzo, Starling, and Revolut allow users to establish savings "spaces" that can be set to invisible or require extra steps for withdrawal, thereby enforcing a form of friction that protects savings without sacrificing usability. These design choices exemplify how technology, when aligned with behavioural insights, can transform saving from a burden into an effortless, even enjoyable, routine.

Real-world examples vividly illustrate the Invisible Account's impact. Take Sarah, a freelance graphic designer with irregular income and numerous financial demands. Previously, Sarah struggled to maintain savings because her funds were commingled with everyday spending money, making it psychologically easier to dip into her "savings" for non-emergencies. After setting up automated transfers into an "invisible" savings pocket—one she deliberately did not display on her app's main screen—she noticed a marked improvement in her ability to accumulate emergency funds. The out-of-sight arrangement reduced temptation and allowed her to "forget" about the savings, only to be pleasantly surprised when reviewing her balances monthly. This stealth saving boosted both her financial buffer and confidence.

Beyond practical mechanics, the Invisible Account trick introduces a layer of *psychological play* to saving. It reframes saving not as a grim sacrifice but as a strategic game of stealth against oneself. This playful framing shifts the emotional valence of saving, transforming it into a challenge that can engage curiosity and foster positive reinforcement. By "hiding" money and observing it grow quietly, savers derive satisfaction not only from the accumulation but from the act of outsmarting their own impulses. This dynamic creates emotional momentum, critical for sustaining saving behaviour over time.

Critically, the Invisible Account strategy must be calibrated to individual circumstances. For some, completely hidden accounts may feel disempowering or disconnected from financial reality, potentially undermining motivation or situational awareness. The hack is most effective when balanced with periodic, intentional engagement—reviewing savings goals and progress without succumbing to impulsive withdrawals. Financial literacy and discipline remain essential companions to automation; the Invisible Account is a tool, not a panacea.

The approach also raises important ethical and systemic considerations. While behavioural hacks can empower individuals, they operate within broader financial ecosystems that often present structural barriers to saving—such as high fees, low interest rates, or limited access to appropriate savings vehicles. Advocacy for more equitable financial products and transparent design complements behavioural strategies, ensuring that innovations like the Invisible Account serve the interests of savers rather than exploiting behavioural vulnerabilities for profit.

From a theoretical standpoint, the Invisible Account aligns with dual-process models of decision-making that distinguish between reflective, deliberate thought and automatic, habitual behaviour. By reducing the need for constant deliberation about saving, the strategy harnesses the power of *automaticity*—embedding saving into routine patterns less susceptible to emotional fluctuation. This cognitive offloading is particularly valuable for those managing complex, unpredictable financial lives, where bandwidth for reflective decision-making is limited.

Furthermore, the Invisible Account trick contributes to reshaping narratives around saving and self-control. Rather than framing saving as an act of willpower prone to failure, it situates saving within *environmental design*—structuring conditions to make desired behaviours easier and default. This shift from moralistic self-discipline to strategic context design reduces shame and fosters sustainable engagement, especially among those for whom saving has historically been fraught or inaccessible.

In practical terms, adopting the Invisible Account approach involves several actionable steps. First, individuals identify or establish dedicated savings accounts or app features separate from primary spending funds. Next, they set up automated transfers timed with income receipt or other triggers, calibrated to manageable amounts. Finally, they adjust visibility settings or use app features to minimise the temptation to access these funds impulsively. Complementary practices include regular, scheduled reviews and framing savings as a protected, untouchable resource designated for specific goals or emergencies.

In sum, the Invisible Account trick represents a powerful convergence of behavioural science, technology, and practical finance. By hiding savings from oneself, individuals harness human psychology's strengths and vulnerabilities, transforming saving from a battleground of temptation into a seamless, stealthy accumulation process. This strategy reintroduces a sense of play and mastery into personal finance, enabling savers to build financial resilience with greater ease and confidence. It exemplifies how thoughtful design and psychological insight can reshape even the most seemingly rigid financial practices into adaptive, empowering habits—pivotal for those embarking on the incremental journey from saving to investing and wealth creation.

Saving Without Shame

Saving money is frequently framed as a straightforward measure of financial discipline, a clear-cut indicator of success or failure. Yet for many—especially those with limited or fluctuating incomes—this framing becomes a source of shame rather than empowerment. The widely held expectation that saving should be regular, substantial, and steady can alienate those whose realities do not align with these ideals. When saving efforts fall short of these norms, individuals often internalise a sense of failure, reinforcing negative self-perceptions and undermining motivation. This chapter challenges these dominant narratives by normalising saving in all its forms, particularly small, irregular amounts, and providing language and frameworks that celebrate these acts as meaningful victories rather than shortcomings. Embracing saving without shame is both a psychological imperative and a practical necessity for fostering sustainable financial wellbeing.

The experience of shame associated with saving—or the lack thereof—has deep roots in social, cultural, and psychological dynamics. Societal narratives valorise financial success as an unequivocal marker of personal worth, often neglecting the structural inequalities and lived complexities that shape individual capacity. This creates a dissonance between aspiration and reality, especially for low-income earners or those navigating precarious work. Financial educators and advisors frequently unintentionally perpetuate these standards by emphasising idealised savings rates or targets without adequate contextualisation. The resultant shame discourages honest engagement with finances and can precipitate withdrawal or avoidance, behaviours that exacerbate financial vulnerability.

Recognising and normalising *small, irregular savings* as valid and valuable disrupts this damaging cycle. Behavioural economics and psychology provide robust evidence that *any* positive saving behaviour, no matter how modest or inconsistent, contributes to building financial identity and momentum. Small wins enhance self-efficacy, fostering motivation and reinforcing the habit loop critical for long-term behaviour change. This understanding reframes savings not as a fixed metric but as a *dynamic process*—a series of incremental acts that cumulatively strengthen financial resilience.

Real-world narratives underscore the transformative impact of this reframing. Consider Jamal, a gig worker with highly variable income who initially viewed his sporadic savings as failures against conventional benchmarks. Upon reframing these irregular deposits as "victories of financial agency," Jamal experienced a profound shift in motivation and confidence. Each small contribution, whether £2 or £20, became a symbol of self-respect and proactive stewardship, countering feelings of scarcity and inadequacy. This narrative shift is crucial, as it aligns financial behaviour with identity in a manner that sustains engagement despite external uncertainty.

This perspective also invites critical reflection on the *moralisation of money*. The tendency to equate saving behaviour with virtue or vice obscures the complex interplay of economic, social, and psychological factors influencing financial capacity. Shame rooted in moral judgement is particularly pernicious because it attacks self-worth rather than behaviour, creating barriers to change. The chapter advocates for a compassionate framework that separates *behavioural assessment* from *personal value*, encouraging individuals to honour their efforts regardless of scale and to view saving as an act of self-care rather than punishment.

Practical strategies for saving without shame involve both cognitive and environmental interventions. On the cognitive front, adopting *non-judgmental self-talk* and recognising the contextual constraints shaping financial decisions reduce internalised stigma. Developing narratives that frame saving as a celebration of possibility—"I saved what I could, and that is progress"—cultivates resilience and optimism. Environmental strategies include setting realistic, flexible goals tailored to fluctuating income, utilising behavioural hacks such as automated micro-savings, and leveraging social support to normalise varied saving patterns.

Technology, too, plays a pivotal role in supporting saving without shame. Apps that allow for irregular, small contributions and that emphasise progress through gamification or positive reinforcement help reorient saving from a burden to a source of satisfaction. Features such as "round-ups," where purchases are rounded to the nearest pound with the difference saved, exemplify how technology can facilitate guilt-free saving by making it effortless and incremental. These innovations embody a behavioural design philosophy that recognises and accommodates human imperfection.

The chapter also addresses potential tensions between celebrating small savings and encouraging ambition. Some critics might argue that normalising modest saving risks complacency or insufficient preparation for financial emergencies. However, the approach presented here does not advocate lowering standards but *recalibrating expectations* to be inclusive and attainable. It recognises that consistent engagement—even at low levels—is a prerequisite for scaling savings over time. By valuing early and imperfect efforts, this framework builds the foundation for more ambitious financial goals, not a substitute for them.

Moreover, saving without shame intersects with broader themes of financial justice and equity. The ability to save is unevenly distributed, influenced by systemic factors such as wage inequality, housing costs, and access to banking. By validating small and irregular savings, this approach counters exclusionary narratives that marginalise those with limited means and challenges the dominant paradigms that equate financial worth with saving volume. It affirms that financial dignity is accessible at all income levels and that every act of saving contributes to personal and communal economic empowerment.

Finally, the emotional dimension of saving without shame extends beyond motivation to encompass *mental health and wellbeing*. Financial stress is a significant contributor to anxiety and depression, and shame compounds this distress by fostering isolation and hopelessness. Embracing saving as a source of pride and agency mitigates these effects, providing psychological refuge and reinforcing a positive self-concept. This holistic view situates saving within a broader framework of self-care and resilience-building.

By reframing saving small, irregular amounts as victories rather than failures, this chapter equips readers with a vital psychological toolkit for sustainable financial engagement. It challenges entrenched narratives, offers compassionate language, and provides practical strategies that align with diverse realities. Embracing saving without shame transforms a frequently fraught financial practice into a source of empowerment, laying the groundwork for confident, consistent wealth-building over a lifetime.

Chapter 4
Investing $5, $50, $500—Designing Your Wealth Thresholds

Investing is often portrayed as an endeavour reserved for those with considerable capital, where the entry points appear prohibitively high. Yet this perception obscures a deeper truth: wealth-building begins not with monumental sums, but with intentional engagement at modest, accessible levels. This chapter invites readers to reconceive investment amounts not as rigid barriers, but as dynamic thresholds—psychological, emotional, and behavioural gateways that mark meaningful inflection points in the journey toward financial identity and agency. By exploring three pivotal tiers—$5, $50, and $500—this chapter provides a framework for establishing personal wealth thresholds that align with individual circumstances, transforming incremental commitment into sustained momentum.

Beginning with five dollars, what may seem inconsequential emerges as a powerful catalyst for change. Micro-investments at this scale, facilitated by fractional share purchasing and microsavings platforms, are far more than financial transactions; they become acts of self-belief and empowerment. Case studies illustrate how regular $5 contributions can reshape mindset—instilling a sense of ownership, participation, and optimism that transcends the nominal amount. These modest commitments lower barriers to entry, making investing approachable for those previously excluded by capital constraints or perceived complexity. The proliferation of fractional shares democratizes access to high-value assets, enabling investors to hold meaningful stakes in companies or funds with minimal capital, redefining conventional ideas of participation.

The $50 tier addresses the common misconception that this sum is "too small to matter." In reality, it functions as a crucial symbol of commitment—a psychological and practical milestone opening doors to broader investment vehicles such as exchange-traded funds (ETFs), robo-advisors, and emerging portfolio strategies. This perspective counters scarcity narratives that erode confidence, framing $50 as a deliberate step in shaping investment identity. The chapter explores how this threshold facilitates diversification, reduces risk, and integrates automated investment tools, providing strategic benefits alongside behavioural reinforcement. Readers receive practical guidance on leveraging this stage to optimise portfolio construction within realistic means.

Reaching the $500 mark invites a more nuanced exploration. Rather than glorifying the amount, the chapter examines the new psychological and practical complexities that accompany larger stakes: heightened responsibility, amplified expectations, and emergent anxieties regarding risk, loss, and performance. Readers are guided in navigating these emotional dynamics, developing risk management strategies, and embracing iterative learning. Here, $500 is positioned not as a destination, but as a transformative rite of passage, deepening financial literacy, confidence, and maturity.

Underlying these tiers is the notion of transformation rites—each dollar threshold represents not merely quantitative growth, but qualitative shifts in behaviour, mindset, and engagement with the financial ecosystem. The chapter draws on psychological theories of identity formation and behavioural change to explain how these milestones serve as markers of investor evolution. Readers are encouraged to document and celebrate these moments, recognising them as sustaining beacons of motivation and resilience.

Throughout, the chapter intertwines practical guidance with philosophical reflection, prompting readers to view investing as a personal, iterative process rather than a distant goal defined by arbitrary sums. It emphasises designing wealth thresholds that are meaningful—tailored to one's context, values, and capacity—thus fostering ownership and reducing intimidation. Technology, behavioural finance, and social narratives are positioned as tools that support investors at each stage, bridging aspiration with action.

Crucially, the chapter situates these thresholds within contemporary financial realities marked by inequality, technological disruption, and shifting labour markets. While acknowledging systemic barriers, it foregrounds individual agency, striking a careful balance between empowerment and realism. Readers gain not only an understanding of investment mechanics but also insight into the broader significance of each tier within socio-economic contexts.

By guiding readers through the deliberate design of their wealth thresholds—from micro-investments to meaningful portfolio engagement—this chapter establishes a foundation for sustained financial growth. It demystifies investing, celebrates incremental progress, and honours the emotional and behavioural dimensions essential to long-term success. In doing so, it transforms investing from an exclusive privilege into an accessible, transformative practice—one dollar threshold at a time.

Five Dollars with a Future

The idea that investing requires large sums of capital has long dominated financial discourse, creating a psychological barrier that discourages many from even starting. Yet the truth is more empowering and accessible: *five dollars a month* can be the seed from which a profound financial identity grows. This seemingly modest amount is not just pocket change—it is a deliberate, symbolic commitment that signals the beginning of a transformative relationship with money. Far from trivial, investing five dollars regularly can spark shifts in mindset, build positive habits, and unlock new opportunities through the rise of fractional shares and microsavings platforms. This chapter explores how small-scale investments carry outsized potential for personal growth and financial inclusion, supported by case studies, modern technology, and behavioural insights.

To understand the significance of investing five dollars, one must first appreciate the psychological dimension of *financial identity*. Investing at any scale is as much about self-perception as it is about portfolio growth. When individuals commit—even modest sums—they enact an identity shift from passive consumer to active investor. This shift alters the internal narrative around money, fostering a sense of agency, responsibility, and future orientation. Studies in behavioural finance underscore this dynamic: the act of investing, rather than the amount invested, is a strong predictor of sustained engagement and wealth-building behaviour. Five dollars is not merely a transaction; it is a statement of intent, a rehearsal of financial self-efficacy.

Emerging financial technologies have democratized the capacity to invest small amounts through *fractional shares*—portions of whole stocks or funds purchasable for minimal sums—and *microsavings platforms* that automate incremental contributions. This technological evolution dismantles traditional barriers of entry, allowing investors with limited capital to access diversified portfolios once out of reach. For example, apps such as Robinhood, Freetrade, and Cash App enable users to buy fractional shares of blue-chip companies, facilitating ownership and participation at unprecedented scales. Simultaneously, microsavings tools aggregate spare change from everyday transactions, funneling it into investment accounts. These innovations translate the abstract concept of investing into concrete, manageable actions aligned with users' financial realities.

Case studies reveal the real-world impact of investing five dollars monthly. Consider Ana, a university student working part-time who began investing five dollars a month through a microsavings app. While her initial financial returns were modest, the behavioural shift was profound. Ana reported increased confidence in financial decision-making, a clearer sense of long-term planning, and motivation to increase contributions as her income grew. Her journey illustrates how small, consistent investments cultivate psychological momentum—often more critical than immediate financial gain. Similarly, Marcus, a gig economy worker, used fractional share platforms to start building a portfolio, experiencing a gradual transformation from viewing money as merely for consumption to regarding it as a tool for growth and security.

However, the simplicity of investing five dollars belies complex conceptual tensions. Critics may argue that such small sums barely register in market returns, questioning the practical value. While it is true that the financial impact may be incremental, the chapter emphasises that investing is a *process* where psychological engagement, habit formation, and identity building are foundational. Financial gains, though important, accrue over time and compound with sustained commitment. Moreover, the act of starting is itself a critical barrier overcome—one that many potential investors never cross due to perceived financial inadequacy or intimidation.

The chapter further explores the structural implications of fractional investing and microsavings. These tools democratise financial markets but also raise ethical and regulatory questions about fees, transparency, and data privacy. Platforms often operate within complex fee structures that may erode returns for small investors, disproportionately impacting those with limited capital. The chapter calls for critical awareness and consumer education to navigate these challenges effectively. It also highlights the importance of policy frameworks that protect small investors and promote equitable access to financial services.

Behavioural science enriches understanding of why five-dollar investments resonate psychologically. Concepts such as *commitment devices* and *loss aversion* explain how small, regular contributions create a sense of obligation and protect against impulsive spending. The visibility of investment growth—even in small amounts—reinforces positive feedback loops, enhancing motivation and financial literacy. By integrating behavioural nudges with technological facilitation, investors harness cognitive and emotional resources essential for long-term wealth-building.

Beyond individual impact, investing five dollars monthly connects to broader themes of financial inclusion and social equity. Historically, participation in capital markets has been restricted by wealth, education, and access. The rise of fractional shares and microsavings platforms signals a shift toward more inclusive financial ecosystems, enabling diverse populations to participate in wealth creation. This democratization challenges entrenched narratives of exclusivity and redefines who can be an investor. Yet, as the chapter underscores, inclusion must be accompanied by empowerment—through education, support, and ethical platform design—to translate access into meaningful outcomes.

Philosophically, the practice of investing small sums invites reflection on the nature of wealth and value. It contests the idea that only large-scale investments confer legitimacy, proposing instead that *wealth-building is a continuum* beginning with intentional acts regardless of scale. This reframing honours the dignity of modest means and the agency embedded in incremental progress. Investing five dollars becomes a *ritual of possibility*, affirming a future-oriented identity that transcends current limitations.

This chapter offers readers not only conceptual frameworks but practical guidance for leveraging five-dollar investments effectively. It discusses selecting appropriate platforms, setting realistic expectations, and integrating investments into broader financial plans. Readers learn how to balance enthusiasm with caution, ambition with patience, and technology use with critical scrutiny. The aim is to equip individuals with the confidence and tools to initiate and sustain their investment journeys, transforming modest contributions into a foundation for enduring financial growth.

In sum, "Five Dollars with a Future" reframes small-scale investing as a profound act of self-transformation and inclusion. It challenges prevailing financial orthodoxies that conflate impact with scale and reframes investing as a human, accessible, and incremental endeavour. Through case studies, behavioural insights, and technological innovations, the chapter illuminates how five dollars a month can ignite identity shifts, build habits, and open doors previously thought closed. This beginning—humble in size but vast in potential—marks the first step toward reclaiming agency and redesigning one's financial future.

$50 as Commitment Energy

In the landscape of personal investing, $50 often occupies a peculiar psychological space. Frequently dismissed as "not enough" to meaningfully participate in markets or build a portfolio, this amount is underestimated in its potential impact. Yet $50 represents more than a mere monetary value—it serves as a critical threshold of *commitment energy*, the symbolic and practical investment that signals a transition from tentative participation to intentional engagement. This chapter reframes $50 not as a limiting factor but as a gateway unlocking access to diversified investment vehicles, automated platforms, and emerging portfolio strategies tailored to the realities of small-scale investors. Understanding $50 as a strategic threshold enables investors to harness behavioural momentum, technological tools, and financial literacy in concert, transforming modest capital into empowered, sustainable action.

The dismissal of $50 as insufficient stems from traditional finance paradigms that equate meaningful investing with large lump sums or complex portfolios. These paradigms often ignore the structural and psychological barriers faced by new or low-income investors. However, behavioural finance research reveals that *commitment*—the act of starting and continuing a practice—is often more determinative of long-term success than initial investment size. When individuals commit $50, they cross a psychological boundary that fosters increased ownership, confidence, and motivation. This act of committing a tangible amount instils a sense of seriousness and identity as an investor, catalysing sustained engagement beyond symbolic participation.

Access to diversified investment options is one of the primary practical benefits unlocked by the $50 threshold. Exchange-traded funds (ETFs), which bundle multiple assets into a single tradable security, have revolutionised portfolio construction by providing low-cost, diversified exposure with relatively low minimum investments. With $50, investors can gain entry into broad market ETFs, sector-specific funds, or socially responsible investment baskets, thereby reducing idiosyncratic risk inherent in single-stock purchases. This diversification is a cornerstone of modern portfolio theory and a critical safeguard for small investors who cannot afford concentrated losses.

Robo-advisors constitute another domain accessible at this level of commitment. These automated platforms offer algorithm-driven portfolio management, dynamically adjusting asset allocation based on risk tolerance, investment horizon, and market conditions. Typically requiring low minimum deposits around or below $50, robo-advisors democratise professional wealth management services that were once exclusive to high-net-worth individuals. The chapter examines how these platforms balance efficiency, cost-effectiveness, and user experience to provide tailored investment solutions that accommodate both novice and seasoned investors. The ease of use and educational resources embedded within robo-advisors further amplify their role in nurturing investor confidence.

Emerging portfolio strategies—such as thematic investing, fractional share acquisition, and socially responsible investing—also become tangible at the $50 threshold. These approaches reflect contemporary shifts in investor values and market innovation. Fractional shares enable investors to own portions of high-priced stocks, removing traditional barriers posed by share price. Thematic investing connects portfolios to specific trends or sectors, aligning financial goals with personal interests or ethical priorities. With $50, investors gain entry into these innovative frameworks, fostering engagement that resonates with identity and values, thereby enhancing motivation and persistence.

Consider the experience of Anita, a part-time teacher who initially perceived investing as out of reach due to limited disposable income. By committing $50 to a diversified ETF portfolio via a robo-advisor, Anita experienced a psychological transformation. The act transcended monetary value; it affirmed her identity as an investor and expanded her financial literacy. Over time, Anita increased contributions, rebalanced portfolios, and engaged actively with investment news. Her case exemplifies how $50 functions as a *commitment catalyst*, initiating behavioural and cognitive shifts essential for long-term wealth-building.

Yet, reaching this threshold also introduces nuanced challenges. Investors may encounter anxiety about market volatility, fear of loss, or imposter syndrome intensified by entry into formal financial markets. The chapter addresses these emotional dimensions, emphasising the importance of realistic expectations, risk education, and incremental learning. It critiques narratives that equate investing with gambling or speculation, advocating for a balanced understanding rooted in disciplined, evidence-based practice. The psychological support and community engagement available through platforms or peer networks are highlighted as critical resources for navigating these early complexities.

The chapter also situates the $50 threshold within broader socioeconomic and technological contexts. It acknowledges that despite lowered minimums, structural inequities persist, including disparities in financial literacy, access to technology, and systemic barriers. Nonetheless, the lowering of financial entry points represents significant progress in financial inclusion, fostering a more diverse investor base. The chapter advocates for continued innovation, policy support, and education to maximise the benefits of these emerging opportunities.

Financial literacy emerges as a vital companion to commitment energy. Understanding fees, asset classes, tax implications, and investment horizons empowers investors to make informed decisions and avoid common pitfalls. The chapter recommends integrating $50 commitments with ongoing education, leveraging resources such as online courses, financial advisors, and interactive tools. This integration ensures that initial commitment evolves into strategic, confident stewardship of financial resources.

Finally, the chapter explores how $50 as commitment energy aligns with broader behavioural principles. It underscores the role of *commitment devices* in overcoming procrastination and inertia, transforming abstract intentions into concrete actions. The threshold acts as a *psychological anchor*—a concrete step that reduces ambiguity and catalyses subsequent investment behaviours. This momentum builds cumulative advantage, illustrating how modest beginnings can yield exponential impact over time.

By reframing $50 from "not enough" to a powerful threshold, this chapter equips readers with a strategic lens and practical toolkit for navigating early-stage investing. It situates modest capital within a framework of agency, accessibility, and growth, revealing how this amount serves as a gateway to diversified portfolios, automated management, and innovative investment vehicles. Through a blend of empirical evidence, case studies, and behavioural insight, readers are empowered to recognise and harness the commitment energy embodied in $50—transforming it into a foundational step toward sustained wealth creation and financial identity development.

What Happens When You Reach $500

Reaching the $500 mark in investing is often celebrated as a milestone—a tangible signal of progress, a threshold of seriousness, or a psychological 'arrival' into the world of wealth-building. Yet this moment, while significant, is far from a simple point of triumph. Rather, it opens a complex terrain of new expectations, emotions, and decisions that many investors are unprepared to navigate. This section critically examines the multifaceted nature of "arriving" at $500, moving beyond surface-level glorification to explore how this threshold reshapes financial identity, introduces new behavioural challenges, and demands evolving strategies. Understanding this complexity is essential for maintaining momentum and fostering a mature, resilient approach to investing.

The symbolic power of $500 cannot be understated. For many emerging investors, accumulating this amount represents a clear departure from the realm of hypothetical or passive saving into active wealth engagement. It signals a transition from tentative experimentation with micro-investments to a portfolio with enough substance to warrant deliberate management. Psychologically, this milestone often intensifies one's self-perception as an investor, bolstering confidence and reinforcing commitment. However, this identity shift also brings heightened scrutiny—both internal and external—as the stakes feel elevated and financial decisions carry greater weight.

This increased gravity introduces a host of emotional complexities. While initial investing may be buoyed by excitement and optimism, reaching $500 can trigger anxiety about potential losses, fear of making mistakes, or pressure to "perform" well. These emotions are rooted in *loss aversion*, a well-documented behavioural bias where the pain of losses outweighs the pleasure of gains, often disproportionately affecting smaller investors. The perceived risk associated with larger sums can lead to paralysis, impulsive decisions, or withdrawal. Recognising and managing these emotional responses is a critical challenge that accompanies this threshold.

The practical implications of $500 as an investment amount are equally intricate. At this level, investors must grapple with portfolio construction, diversification, and fees in ways less relevant at micro-investment scales. The choice between individual stocks, exchange-traded funds (ETFs), bonds, or other instruments becomes more pressing, as does consideration of cost-efficiency and tax implications. Transaction fees, which might have been negligible with smaller trades, can materially affect returns. This complexity requires a leap in financial literacy and engagement, necessitating deliberate learning or advisory support to optimise outcomes.

Case studies exemplify the dual nature of this milestone. Take Jamal, who diligently built his portfolio to $500 through consistent micro-investing. Upon reaching this amount, Jamal found himself uncertain whether to consolidate holdings, diversify further, or exit certain positions. The novelty of these decisions introduced stress and hesitation, prompting a temporary disengagement from investing. Conversely, Maya, upon reaching the same threshold, leveraged the moment to deepen her financial education, rebalanced her portfolio with the aid of a robo-advisor, and set clear, incremental goals for continued growth. These contrasting experiences illustrate that reaching $500 is not an endpoint but a *critical juncture* requiring strategic adjustment and psychological readiness.

This juncture also brings forward the tension between *aspiration and realism.* On one hand, $500 feels significant enough to warrant ambitious growth strategies; on the other, it remains a relatively modest sum in the context of long-term financial goals such as retirement or homeownership. Managing expectations—both personal and societal—is vital to sustaining motivation and preventing disillusionment. The chapter explores how calibrating goals to reflect realistic time horizons, risk tolerance, and income trajectories fosters balanced decision-making and resilience.

The arrival at $500 also invites reflection on behavioural patterns established during earlier investing stages. Habits of consistency, patience, and learning become increasingly consequential as portfolios grow. Conversely, tendencies toward impulsivity or neglect can become more costly. This threshold therefore serves as a litmus test for behavioural maturity, highlighting areas for growth or recalibration. Integrating tools such as periodic portfolio reviews, automated contributions, and educational resources supports the development of sustainable investing behaviours aligned with evolving financial identity.

Importantly, the chapter situates the $500 milestone within broader systemic and cultural contexts. Economic inequality, access to financial services, and cultural attitudes toward money influence how this threshold is experienced and negotiated. For some, reaching $500 may be a remarkable achievement reflecting overcoming structural barriers; for others, it may be a routine step in wealth-building. Understanding these contexts enriches the investor's perspective, fostering empathy and reducing unproductive comparisons or stigma.

Technological advancements play a significant role at this stage. Digital platforms increasingly offer sophisticated yet accessible tools that assist investors in managing portfolios at this scale—ranging from robo-advisors providing automated diversification to educational dashboards visualising progress and risk. These tools help bridge knowledge gaps and lower barriers to informed decision-making. However, the chapter emphasises the need for critical engagement with technology, avoiding overreliance or passive use, and advocating for digital literacy as an ongoing practice.

The ethical dimension of arriving at $500 includes considerations of transparency, fees, and fiduciary responsibility. Investors must navigate a financial ecosystem where conflicts of interest, opaque costs, and marketing pressures abound. Empowering investors with knowledge about these issues is crucial to protecting their capital and trust. This chapter highlights strategies for vetting platforms, understanding fee structures, and recognising predatory practices that disproportionately affect smaller investors.

Philosophically, reaching $500 challenges simplistic narratives of linear progress in investing. Instead, it reveals the *nonlinear, iterative nature* of financial growth, marked by periods of uncertainty, learning, and adaptation. This perspective encourages investors to view milestones as part of a dynamic process rather than fixed endpoints, cultivating patience and openness to evolving strategies and identities.

In navigating what happens when $500 is reached, investors engage with a complex interplay of emotion, strategy, identity, and context. This chapter provides a nuanced roadmap that moves beyond celebration to critical preparation, equipping readers to embrace this threshold with confidence and clarity. It invites a reconceptualisation of milestones as transformation rites—moments that demand reflection, recalibration, and renewed commitment—laying the foundation for sustained, intentional wealth-building.

Thresholds as Transformation Rites

Financial milestones—whether $5, $50, or $500—are often regarded simply as quantitative markers: measures of capital accumulated, stepping stones toward wealth. Yet to perceive these thresholds purely in numerical terms is to overlook their profound emotional and behavioural significance. Each new dollar tier functions as a *transformation rite*, a symbolic and psychological passage that reshapes identity, alters habits, and deepens commitment to the financial journey. This chapter explores how crossing these thresholds catalyses not only economic growth but also fundamental shifts in self-perception and action, revealing investing as an evolving practice grounded in ritual and meaning rather than mere arithmetic.

The concept of thresholds as rites of passage draws from anthropological and psychological theories that view human development as punctuated by ritualised transitions. These rituals mark shifts in status, responsibility, and worldview—effects mirrored in the investor's experience of crossing new financial tiers. When an individual moves from tentative micro-investing to a sustained $50 commitment, or from cautious accumulation to a $500 portfolio, they are not just amassing assets but undergoing *identity recalibration.* The act of reaching a threshold instantiates a new self-narrative: from bystander to participant, from consumer to steward. This narrative realignment fundamentally influences behaviour, motivation, and resilience.

Emotional complexity accompanies these transitions. Early thresholds often evoke exhilaration and validation—"I am really an investor now"—but also uncertainty and vulnerability. The stakes feel higher; fear of loss, impostor syndrome, or anxiety about market fluctuations intensify. These affective states are integral to the rite, functioning as catalysts for growth by compelling reflection and adaptation. For example, reaching a $500 portfolio might prompt an investor to confront their risk tolerance more honestly, seek education, or engage advisors, thereby deepening financial competence and confidence. Rather than obstacles, these emotional responses serve as *transformative pressures* that shape investor maturation.

Behavioural shifts at thresholds manifest in habits and decision-making patterns. Initial investments may be sporadic and exploratory; crossing tiers often demands discipline, routine, and strategic planning. Automated contributions, portfolio rebalancing, and goal-setting become salient practices. These behavioural adaptations reinforce the evolving financial identity, creating feedback loops where new actions consolidate the psychological shifts prompted by thresholds. The chapter draws on habit formation theory to elucidate how ritualised financial behaviours are essential to sustaining momentum beyond initial enthusiasm.

Case studies illuminate these dynamics vividly. Consider Leah, who viewed her first $5 investment as symbolic but inconsequential. Upon consistently investing and reaching the $50 tier, Leah experienced a profound sense of agency and responsibility. This milestone motivated her to learn about ETFs, automate contributions, and articulate long-term goals. Crossing into the $500 range brought new challenges—managing portfolio diversification and confronting market volatility—but also deepened her identification as an investor. Leah's narrative exemplifies how thresholds trigger layered transformations, encompassing cognition, emotion, and behaviour.

Contrasting experiences reveal that thresholds are not universally empowering. For some, crossing tiers can precipitate stress, self-doubt, or decision paralysis, especially in the absence of supportive knowledge or community. This underscores the chapter's emphasis on *contextualising rites*—recognising that thresholds interact with personal histories, social environments, and structural factors. The rites are not magical cures but moments requiring scaffolding through education, mentorship, and empathetic guidance. Appreciating this complexity avoids simplistic triumphalism and promotes inclusive financial empowerment.

Technological tools mediate many contemporary threshold experiences. Digital platforms offering fractional shares, robo-advisors, and educational resources facilitate smooth transitions by reducing cognitive burdens and providing instant feedback. However, overreliance on technology risks detaching investors from the reflective practices essential to transformation. The chapter advocates for *intentional engagement*—using technology as a catalyst rather than a crutch—and emphasises the cultivation of critical thinking alongside convenience.

Philosophically, viewing thresholds as transformation rites challenges dominant narratives of investing as a purely economic endeavour. It situates wealth-building within *human developmental processes* involving meaning-making, identity construction, and emotional regulation. This reframing humanises investing, acknowledging that financial growth is inseparable from psychological and social dimensions. It invites investors to approach thresholds as invitations to self-discovery and personal growth, enriching the material gains with deeper purpose.

The chapter further interrogates cultural narratives around money and success that influence threshold experiences. Societal messages often valorise linear progress, quick wins, and large-scale accumulation, marginalising incremental and process-oriented perspectives. Embracing thresholds as rites disrupts these narratives by honouring gradual transformation and recognising the legitimacy of diverse financial journeys. This perspective fosters dignity and patience, crucial for investors navigating volatility and uncertainty.

In practice, recognising thresholds as transformation rites invites deliberate rituals and reflective practices. Journaling milestones, celebrating progress, engaging in peer discussions, and revisiting goals become tools for embedding psychological shifts. These rituals create *psychosocial anchors* that stabilise identity amid the fluidity of markets and personal circumstances. By ritualising thresholds, investors reinforce their evolving relationship with money and commitment to sustained growth.

In sum, thresholds in investing are far more than fiscal markers; they are profound rites of passage that shape who investors become and how they act. This chapter provides a rigorous, nuanced exploration of these transformations, integrating behavioural science, anthropology, and real-world narratives to illuminate the emotional and behavioural landscape of wealth thresholds. Understanding and embracing these rites equips readers to navigate financial growth with wisdom, resilience, and intentionality—transforming incremental dollars into enduring change.

Chapter 5
The Habit Architecture of Everyday Investing

Investing is frequently imagined as a sporadic, high-stakes endeavour—something to be attempted only during fleeting moments of financial stability or opportune market conditions. Yet for those managing modest means or irregular incomes, meaningful wealth emerges not from intermittent bursts of effort but from the careful cultivation of consistent, sustainable habits. This chapter delves into the architecture of everyday investing, illustrating how psychologically attuned routines transform what might otherwise feel like a burdensome task into an integrated, identity-affirming practice. Moving beyond mere repetition, it frames investment as a ritualised act—a disciplined yet deeply personal engagement that anchors financial behaviour in self-concept rather than obligation.

The distinction between ritual and routine is crucial. Routines often feel mechanical, imposed by external demands or sheer force of will. Rituals, by contrast, are suffused with intention and meaning. By ritualising investment, each action becomes a reaffirmation of values and a projection of future vision. This subtle shift—from obligation to identity—diminishes resistance and fosters resilience, transforming investing from a chore into a source of pride and agency. Drawing on habit psychology and identity theory, the chapter explores methods to deliberately cultivate and sustain this transformation, particularly for those operating at a small-scale or irregular investing cadence.

Central to embedding this ritual is the use of trigger systems—practical mechanisms that link investment behaviours to existing habits, life events, or environmental cues. Rather than relying on fragile willpower, triggers leverage automaticity, aligning contributions with familiar routines: a post-payday allocation, a calendar-based reminder, or the habit of rounding up transactions for investment. These anchors reduce cognitive load and decision fatigue, allowing investment to become a seamless, habitual response rather than a daily negotiation. The chapter offers step-by-step guidance for identifying and implementing triggers suitable to diverse lifestyles.

Equally significant is the approach to monitoring progress. Traditional financial tracking can provoke anxiety or guilt, especially when targets are missed or returns fluctuate. To counter this, the chapter introduces journaling and visualisation techniques that transform tracking into a reflective, almost artistic exercise—celebrating incremental progress, contextualising setbacks, and fostering emotional engagement. This reframing nurtures positive feedback loops that reinforce commitment and psychological wellbeing, challenging deficit-focused financial narratives while providing personalised, motivating systems for readers to follow.

The inevitability of imperfection is embraced with deliberate care. Skipping a month of contributions is not failure but an opportunity for adaptive learning. The chapter provides compassionate frameworks for responding to setbacks without guilt, emphasising process over perfection. Practical cognitive scripts and reframes empower investors to re-engage confidently after lapses, normalising imperfection as an integral part of sustainable habit formation. This orientation reduces burnout while cultivating persistence—a vital quality when navigating the unpredictability of income and life.

Throughout, the chapter weaves together behavioural science, real-world case studies, and philosophical reflection to construct a robust model of everyday investing. It recognises the emotional, cognitive, and contextual complexities influencing financial behaviour and offers actionable strategies grounded in lived experience. Common barriers—procrastination, self-doubt, financial anxiety—are addressed directly, demonstrating how habit architecture provides durable solutions anchored in identity and meaning.

Moreover, the chapter situates habit formation within broader socio-economic realities, acknowledging that systemic factors shape both capacity and opportunity. It advocates for adaptive, context-sensitive approaches that respect diverse income patterns, cultural attitudes, and resource access. This inclusive stance ensures that the proposed habit framework is flexible, not prescriptive, and adaptable to varying circumstances.

Readers are also encouraged to reflect on how their financial practices intersect with personal values, aspirations, and self-conception. This integration elevates habit architecture from mechanical repetition to a coherent, identity-affirming journey. Investing thus emerges not merely as a financial action but as a lived philosophy—a daily expression of agency, foresight, and intention.

This chapter sets the stage for a reimagining of everyday investing. It presents evidence-based insights into how ritual, triggers, tracking, and emotional flexibility combine into sustainable habits. Readers will gain the tools and understanding necessary to build investment behaviours that feel natural, rewarding, and aligned with their evolving identities, empowering them to navigate the complexities of financial growth with both confidence and composure.

How to Build a Ritual, Not a Routine

The difference between a routine and a ritual lies not in the actions themselves, but in the meaning they carry and the role they play in shaping identity. When it comes to investing, this distinction is crucial. Too often, investing is approached as a mundane obligation—a checkbox to be ticked amid competing priorities—leading to disengagement, inconsistency, and emotional fatigue. By contrast, ritualising investment transforms it into a meaningful act aligned with one's values and self-concept, fostering enduring commitment and psychological resilience. This chapter delves into the science and art of building investing rituals, drawing on habit psychology and identity theory to illuminate how investors can cultivate practices that are both sustainable and identity-affirming.

At the core of this transformation is the understanding that habits anchored solely in external obligation tend to falter under stress or disruption. Habit psychology reveals that behaviours reinforced by internal motivation and identity integration exhibit greater stability over time. Rituals, by embedding action within a narrative of who one is or aspires to be, harness intrinsic motivation and emotional engagement. Investing, when ritualised, becomes a daily affirmation of agency and future orientation—a declaration that financial stewardship is not a chore but a core part of selfhood. This shift radically changes the quality of engagement, encouraging perseverance through setbacks and fluctuations.

Consider the example of Thomas, who initially treated investing as a task to complete when convenient, resulting in erratic contributions and growing frustration. Upon reframing investment as a ritual—his "morning financial meditation"—linked to his identity as a responsible provider and planner, Thomas developed a disciplined, joyful practice. This ritual involved a brief, mindful review of his portfolio each payday, coupled with a small automated transfer. The act transcended mechanics, becoming a moment of connection with his values and goals. Over time, this ritual strengthened his confidence and reduced anxiety, illustrating how ritualising behaviour fosters both consistency and psychological wellbeing.

The chapter explores practical strategies for constructing investing rituals that resonate personally. Key among these is *intentionality*: explicitly linking investment actions to identity statements or affirmations—such as "I am an investor building security for my family"—that contextualise behaviour within a larger narrative. This approach aligns with self-determination theory, which emphasises autonomy, competence, and relatedness as motivators for sustained behaviour. Rituals also benefit from sensory or symbolic elements—such as lighting a candle, playing specific music, or using a dedicated journal—that enhance emotional salience and memory encoding.

Moreover, ritualising investment involves *temporal and spatial structuring*. Anchoring investment acts to specific times (e.g., morning coffee) or places (e.g., a particular chair) creates environmental cues that facilitate habit formation and reinforce meaning. This spatial-temporal framework supports automaticity while preserving the ritual's intentional and reflective qualities. The chapter integrates insights from neuroscience demonstrating how rituals engage brain networks linked to reward and identity, strengthening neural pathways associated with the behaviour.

The tension between ritual and routine emerges as a central theme. Routines may rely on repetition but often lack emotional depth, leading to disengagement. Rituals demand greater cognitive and emotional investment but yield richer psychological rewards. The chapter interrogates how investors can balance these demands, employing rituals to anchor core practices while allowing flexibility to accommodate life's unpredictability. This balance prevents ritual burnout and supports long-term sustainability.

Technology's role in supporting investing rituals is also examined. Financial apps, alerts, and automated transfers can be integrated into rituals, providing structure without sacrificing personal meaning. However, overreliance on automation risks diminishing the ritual's intentionality; thus, mindful engagement remains essential. The chapter encourages combining technological convenience with reflective practices—such as journaling or goal visualization—to maintain emotional connection and ownership.

Critically, the chapter situates ritualising investment within broader cultural and social contexts. Rituals have historically served communal and identity functions; their contemporary adaptation to personal finance reflects shifting relationships with money, autonomy, and future planning. Recognising these cultural dimensions enriches understanding and highlights opportunities for collective rituals—such as investment clubs or shared goal-setting—that amplify motivation and social support.

Ethical reflection underscores that ritualising investment should not obscure systemic barriers or individual constraints. The chapter advocates for compassionate, context-sensitive application, honouring diverse financial realities and discouraging rigid prescription. Rituals must empower without imposing, adapt without alienating.

By inviting readers to build investing rituals rather than mere routines, this chapter offers a paradigm shift—one that transforms investment from a mechanical task into a purposeful, identity-affirming practice. It provides evidence-based strategies, real-world examples, and nuanced analysis to guide the creation of habits that endure, enrich, and empower. Through ritual, investing becomes not only a path to financial growth but a daily act of self-respect and intentional living.

Trigger Systems, Not Willpower

The popular narrative of self-control often venerates willpower as the central force behind successful behaviour change. Yet a vast body of behavioural science reveals a far more reliable pathway: designing *trigger systems* that anchor desired actions—such as investing—into existing habits, cues, or life events. This insight is especially crucial for everyday investors who juggle limited time, fluctuating income, and competing priorities. Rather than relying on the fragile, often exhausting resource of willpower, the most effective investment behaviours emerge when they are embedded within a network of contextual triggers that prompt automatic, consistent action. This chapter unpacks practical methods to harness trigger systems, illustrating how small design choices in habit formation can transform investing from sporadic effort into seamless, sustained practice.

At the heart of trigger systems lies the recognition that human behaviour is largely habitual, operating on automatic responses to environmental cues. Classic psychological research—such as Charles Duhigg's exploration of the habit loop—demonstrates that behaviours are initiated by triggers, followed by routine execution and a subsequent reward. Effective habit formation capitalises on this sequence by deliberately pairing new behaviours with well-established triggers, thereby reducing cognitive friction and bypassing the need for conscious motivation. In the context of investing, this means that instead of trying to summon willpower to act, investors link investing activities to stable routines or meaningful life events, creating dependable pathways to action.

Anchoring investment behaviour to existing habits is a practical starting point. For example, coupling investment contributions with the routine of receiving a paycheck leverages a fixed temporal trigger, ensuring that the act of investing is part of the natural financial rhythm rather than an optional decision. Similarly, pairing investment reviews with habitual activities—such as morning coffee or Sunday planning—builds consistency through contextual cues. The chapter explores case studies where investors who incorporated investing into existing behavioural clusters experienced significant improvements in contribution regularity and engagement, underscoring the power of contextual alignment.

Life events offer another potent category of triggers. Events such as tax refunds, bonuses, or milestone birthdays can serve as inflection points to initiate or boost investment activity. These events carry emotional and financial salience, making them ideal moments to reinforce investment behaviours. Moreover, the chapter discusses how even less predictable triggers—like receiving a payment from gig work or achieving a fitness goal—can be repurposed as prompts for investing. This flexible approach recognises the diversity of income streams and lifestyles, especially relevant for non-traditional earners.

Beyond temporal and event-based triggers, environmental design plays a crucial role. Physical and digital cues—such as placing investment reminders on frequently viewed screens, scheduling calendar alerts, or configuring app notifications—serve as external scaffolding to support trigger-response behaviour. However, the chapter cautions against over-reliance on intrusive reminders, advocating instead for thoughtfully integrated cues that harmonise with the individual's routines and preferences. Balancing visibility with subtlety enhances adherence without generating notification fatigue or resistance.

The distinction between triggers and willpower carries important ethical and psychological implications. While willpower is finite and prone to depletion, triggers operate by reshaping the behavioural landscape, reducing the cognitive and emotional burden of decision-making. This shift aligns with contemporary models of self-regulation that emphasise *choice architecture* and *environmental shaping* over moralistic notions of self-discipline. For investors, this means designing systems that respect human limitations and harness automaticity rather than demanding heroic exertion.

Yet trigger systems are not foolproof. They require careful calibration and reinforcement. The chapter addresses challenges such as trigger fatigue, context changes, and the need for ongoing adaptation. For instance, life transitions—changing jobs, moving, or shifting schedules—can disrupt established triggers, necessitating conscious redesign. The role of *meta-cognition*—awareness and reflection on one's habits—is highlighted as essential for maintaining and evolving trigger systems over time.

Critically, the chapter situates trigger systems within broader behavioural frameworks, including *implementation intentions*—the mental planning of "if-then" scenarios that link cues to actions. This technique strengthens trigger-response connections and prepares individuals to navigate obstacles. Research evidence supporting implementation intentions in financial behaviour is reviewed, providing a robust scientific foundation for practical application.

The chapter also acknowledges the interplay between individual agency and systemic factors. While triggers can empower behaviour change, structural barriers such as income volatility, access to financial products, and digital literacy influence the feasibility of establishing and sustaining investment habits. The discussion integrates socio-economic considerations, advocating for trigger systems as one element within a comprehensive approach to financial inclusion.

Real-world applications illustrate the diverse modalities of trigger systems. For example, a freelancer who invests a fixed percentage of each payment automatically capitalises on income-linked triggers, reducing reliance on willpower. Another case involves a parent who ties investment reviews to weekly family meetings, embedding financial stewardship within relational rhythms. These examples demonstrate the adaptability of trigger design to varied contexts and values.

Technology's role is explored with nuance. Digital tools facilitate sophisticated trigger systems through automation, reminders, and data visualisation, but the chapter stresses that technology must be personalised and integrated thoughtfully to avoid alienation or overwhelm. Combining digital triggers with tactile rituals or social accountability can enhance effectiveness and emotional resonance.

Philosophically, embracing trigger systems invites a shift from viewing investing as a series of discrete, effortful acts toward perceiving it as an emergent property of well-structured behavioural ecosystems. This perspective aligns investing with lived experience and human nature, fostering compassion and practicality in habit formation.

By focusing on trigger systems rather than willpower, this chapter provides readers with actionable, research-backed strategies to anchor investing in everyday life. It empowers individuals to design contexts that support automatic, joyful engagement with their financial futures—transforming investment from a taxing obligation into a natural, integrated practice.

Tracking that Feels Like Art, Not Guilt

The act of tracking one's investment progress is widely regarded as a fundamental component of effective financial management. Yet, for many, this practice evokes a complex emotional response—shame, anxiety, and self-criticism often accompany even the most diligent record-keeping. Traditional financial tracking tools, with their sterile numbers and relentless comparisons, can reduce deeply personal journeys into mechanical scoreboards of success or failure. This emotional landscape risks alienating investors, particularly those navigating small or inconsistent contributions, who may perceive setbacks as personal inadequacies. This chapter reimagines tracking as an *artful, empowering practice*—one that fosters reflection, celebrates progress, and invites growth without guilt. It introduces innovative journaling and visual methods that transform tracking from a punitive obligation into a source of motivation and self-understanding.

The emotional toll of conventional financial tracking deserves close attention. Research in behavioural economics and psychology reveals that negative affect associated with tracking can trigger avoidance behaviours, undermine motivation, and exacerbate financial stress. The problem is compounded by the social and cultural narratives that equate wealth with worth, turning numbers into harsh verdicts on identity and effort. This chapter interrogates these dynamics, arguing that guilt-infused tracking is counterproductive and proposing alternative models that honour the investor's experience with nuance and compassion.

Innovative journaling techniques provide one avenue for transforming tracking into a creative, reflective process. Rather than focusing solely on quantitative metrics—such as portfolio value or monthly returns—these methods encourage narrative exploration of emotional responses, challenges overcome, and lessons learned. For example, investors might write brief entries following each contribution or review session, capturing thoughts about what the act of investing means to them, how it aligns with their values, or what obstacles they faced. This narrative journaling supports metacognition, helping investors externalise and process feelings, thereby reducing shame and fostering resilience.

Visual tools amplify the emotional and cognitive benefits of alternative tracking. Graphical representations—such as progress maps, colour-coded calendars, or investment mood charts—enable investors to see their journey as a dynamic, evolving artwork rather than a static ledger. These visualisations invite playful engagement and reinterpret fluctuations not as failures but as textured variations contributing to a larger story. Digital platforms increasingly incorporate such features, allowing personalisation and interactive exploration. The chapter evaluates a range of visual tracking modalities, assessing their psychological impact and practical utility.

Crucially, the chapter addresses the tension between transparency and compassion in tracking. While honesty about financial realities is essential, it must be balanced with kindness toward oneself. Tracking that emphasises growth, effort, and intention over rigid benchmarks encourages a growth mindset, which research associates with improved long-term outcomes. The chapter presents frameworks for cultivating this mindset through tracking, including affirmations, gratitude practices, and recognition of incremental progress.

Case studies illustrate the transformative potential of artful tracking. Sarah, a freelance writer with fluctuating income, adopted a combined narrative and visual journal to document her investment journey. Over time, she reported increased confidence, reduced anxiety, and a stronger sense of agency. Another example features David, who used a colour-coded calendar system to celebrate weeks of consistent investing, reframing minor lapses as opportunities for renewal rather than failure. These real-world stories highlight how reframing tracking practices can break cycles of shame and disengagement.

The chapter also explores cultural dimensions influencing tracking experiences. In cultures where financial discussion is taboo or where scarcity narratives prevail, shame around tracking may be amplified. Addressing these contexts requires sensitivity and adaptation, incorporating community narratives and collective support structures that normalise financial reflection and reduce isolation. The potential of group journaling or peer tracking initiatives to foster accountability and shared learning is examined as a promising avenue.

Technological innovation offers both opportunities and challenges for reimagined tracking. Mobile apps and platforms increasingly integrate features that support positive emotional engagement—such as personalised milestones, encouraging notifications, and adaptive visualisations. However, the chapter warns against over-reliance on gamification or surface-level rewards that may trivialise the depth of financial growth. Instead, it advocates for thoughtful design that respects the investor's complexity and promotes sustained, meaningful interaction.

Ethical considerations surface around data privacy and the psychological effects of constant monitoring. The chapter urges critical awareness and informed consent in adopting tracking tools, empowering investors to choose methods aligned with their values and wellbeing.

Philosophically, transforming tracking from guilt to art reframes investing as a human, embodied practice—a dialogue between self, values, and future. This perspective challenges reductive notions of finance as cold calculation, restoring dignity and emotional richness to the financial journey.

By embracing innovative, compassionate tracking methods, investors can cultivate a sustainable relationship with their portfolios—one that honours progress, nurtures learning, and transcends punitive metrics. This chapter equips readers with evidence-based strategies and inspiring examples to redesign tracking as a practice of empowerment and self-discovery, fostering financial growth that feels not like a burden, but like art.

What to Do When You Miss a Month: Teaching Emotional Flexibility, Not Perfectionism

Missing a month of investing can feel like a setback that threatens the hard-earned momentum of financial discipline. For many, this experience provokes a cascade of negative emotions: guilt, shame, frustration, and self-reproach. These feelings are compounded by societal expectations that frame investing as a domain of unwavering commitment and flawless execution. Yet, insisting on perfection is not only unrealistic but counterproductive; it can erode motivation, foster anxiety, and ultimately sabotage long-term progress. This chapter advocates a radically different approach—embracing *emotional flexibility* as the key to sustainable investing. By cultivating compassion, resilience, and adaptive strategies, investors learn to navigate lapses without derailment, transforming missed months from sources of shame into opportunities for growth and renewal.

The psychological impact of missing an investment contribution is profound, particularly for those living with tight budgets or irregular incomes. The *all-or-nothing mindset*—a common cognitive distortion—intensifies feelings of failure, prompting some to abandon their investment plans entirely. Behavioural research highlights how this perfectionistic thinking undermines habit formation and self-efficacy. Conversely, adopting a flexible mindset allows investors to contextualise lapses within the broader trajectory of their financial journey, maintaining engagement despite imperfections. This shift in perspective reframes missed months not as catastrophic failures but as natural, expected variations in a complex process.

Central to emotional flexibility is the practice of *self-compassion*, a concept extensively studied in psychological science. Self-compassion involves treating oneself with kindness and understanding in moments of difficulty rather than harsh judgement. In the context of missed investments, self-compassion mitigates the harsh internal dialogue that fuels guilt and shame. It encourages recognition that financial behaviour occurs within a web of external constraints, personal circumstances, and systemic factors often beyond individual control. This compassionate stance fosters psychological safety, empowering investors to recommit without fear or self-punishment.

Practical strategies for cultivating emotional flexibility include cognitive reframing techniques. For instance, rather than interpreting a missed month as "I failed," an investor might reframe it as "This is a temporary setback, and I have the capacity to resume." Such reframing draws on principles of cognitive-behavioural therapy and has been shown to improve motivation and reduce avoidance. The chapter offers scripts and reflective prompts to assist readers in developing these adaptive narratives, emphasizing the power of language in shaping emotional experience.

Another key aspect is *normalising imperfection* within investment communities. Sharing stories of lapses and recoveries combats isolation and stigma, building communal resilience. Platforms and peer groups that encourage openness about setbacks cultivate supportive environments where emotional flexibility can flourish. The chapter reviews examples of investment forums and social initiatives that successfully integrate this ethos, illustrating how collective vulnerability strengthens individual persistence.

Technological tools also play a role in supporting emotional flexibility. Automated contributions and "catch-up" features allow investors to resume or compensate for missed months with minimal friction. Notifications and reminders can be framed positively, offering encouragement rather than reproach. However, the chapter cautions against over-dependence on technology to manage emotions, underscoring the necessity of internal coping skills and reflective practice.

Financial education emerges as a foundational pillar. Understanding market volatility, long-term growth patterns, and the non-linear nature of investing helps set realistic expectations that buffer against perfectionism. Educators and advisors are encouraged to integrate emotional literacy into financial guidance, preparing investors to handle setbacks with equanimity.

The chapter further explores the ethical dimension of emotional flexibility. It challenges societal narratives that equate financial success with moral worth, highlighting how these narratives perpetuate exclusion and distress. By promoting kindness and patience, the approach aligns investing with holistic wellbeing rather than narrow performance metrics.

Philosophically, embracing emotional flexibility situates investing within *human developmental frameworks* that value learning through trial, error, and adaptation. This view honours the complexity of life's uncertainties and the inevitability of imperfection, positioning resilience as a core investment asset.

Through illustrative case studies, readers encounter individuals who have transformed missed contributions into moments of insight and recommitment. For example, Maria, a gig economy worker, shares how reframing missed months as part of her unique financial rhythm preserved her motivation and ultimately strengthened her investment practice. These narratives exemplify the principles of emotional flexibility in action.

By prioritising emotional flexibility over perfectionism, this chapter equips readers with a compassionate, pragmatic toolkit to sustain investment habits in the face of inevitable disruptions. It invites a redefinition of success—not as flawless adherence but as *persistent engagement* marked by grace, learning, and renewed intention. In doing so, it transforms the experience of missing a month from a source of guilt into a catalyst for deeper financial and personal growth.

Chapter 6
Fragments of Ownership—How to Invest Without Buying Whole Things

The world of investing has quietly shifted, dismantling barriers that once reserved asset ownership for the affluent. Today, technological advances and the democratization of finance have created a new paradigm: owning fractions of high-value assets rather than entire shares or properties. This chapter examines how fractional ownership—through fractional shares, exchange-traded funds (ETFs), and emerging digital instruments such as cryptocurrencies—redefines access, agency, and strategy for investors with modest means. It encourages readers to reconsider the meaning of ownership in the modern era, demonstrating how micro-investments, when executed thoughtfully, can deliver disproportionate psychological and financial benefits.

At the core of this evolution lies fractional shares, which divide expensive stocks—once accessible only to the wealthy—into affordable portions. Platforms such as Robinhood, Fidelity, and M1 Finance now enable investors to acquire slices of companies like Amazon or Tesla for just a few dollars. By lowering the entry point, these tools permit participation in markets historically barred by prohibitive prices. The chapter delves into the mechanics of fractional shares, addressing common misconceptions around ownership, dividends, and voting rights. Crucially, fractional investing is portrayed not as a mere technical convenience but as a vehicle for financial identity formation, fostering a tangible sense of engagement and belonging within the market.

Alongside fractional shares, ETFs offer indispensable support to those seeking diversification without complexity. Often misunderstood, ETFs provide low-cost exposure to a broad range of assets—from global equities to bonds, sectors, or thematic strategies. This chapter demystifies ETFs in accessible language, illustrating how even modest contributions can achieve diversification traditionally reserved for institutional investors. Through examples and comparative analysis, it demonstrates how

ETFs reduce risk, simplify portfolio management, and serve as scalable building blocks for long-term wealth accumulation, making them particularly suited for investors navigating fragmented ownership.

The discussion then turns to cryptocurrency, frequently depicted as a volatile frontier of investment. While crypto assets carry high risk and speculation, the chapter reframes small-scale crypto investments—as low as $10—not as reckless wagers but as exercises in financial literacy, risk awareness, and technological fluency. Drawing on behavioural finance and educational psychology, it presents micro-investments in crypto as laboratories for experiential learning, allowing investors to understand market dynamics and cultivate emotional resilience. Enthusiasm for innovation is tempered with careful attention to regulatory uncertainty, ethical considerations, and the importance of intentional, informed participation.

A central theme emphasises the distinction between genuine ownership and gambling. Even small investments in fractional shares, ETFs, or crypto can excite emotionally, potentially obscuring rational decision-making. The chapter equips readers with tools to evaluate whether investment behaviour contributes to long-term value or merely fuels short-term thrill. Drawing on behavioural research—overconfidence, herd behaviour, and loss aversion—it introduces practical heuristics and reflective prompts that encourage mindful, disciplined investing, resisting the allure of "get rich quick" narratives.

Fragmented ownership also invites philosophical reflection. What does it mean to hold a fraction of a corporation or digital token? How do such holdings shape one's relationship with markets, society, and self? By integrating perspectives from economic sociology and ethics, the chapter explores both empowering potentials and nuanced complexities, linking practical guidance to a deeper understanding of the socio-cultural implications of fractional ownership.

Technology underpins much of this accessibility, but the chapter cautions against uncritical reliance. It examines platform limitations, hidden costs, data privacy concerns, and the risks of dependency, providing strategies to vet providers, safeguard assets, and maintain autonomy in the digital ecosystem.

Case studies bring theory to life: a young professional building a diversified portfolio via micro-investing apps; a retiree cautiously using ETFs for income stability; a novice experimenting with small crypto positions. These narratives illustrate how fragments of ownership can act as seeds for financial agency, identity development, and enduring wealth practices.

By exploring fractional shares, ETFs, and cryptocurrencies in an integrated framework, this chapter empowers readers to navigate modern investment landscapes with confidence and discernment. It frames fragmented ownership not as a compromise, but as a revolutionary expansion of access—one that democratizes wealth-building and reshapes the concept of what it means to be an investor in the twenty-first century.

Fractional Shares: The New Doorway

Investing has long been perceived as an arena reserved for those with substantial capital, where owning even a single share of prominent companies like Amazon, Google, or Tesla required a significant financial outlay. This barrier, rooted in the traditional mechanics of stock ownership, has historically limited participation to affluent investors or those willing to pool resources extensively. Yet, a fundamental shift has taken place in recent years, catalysed by technological innovation and regulatory evolution: the advent of *fractional shares*. This development dismantles the old paradigm by allowing individuals to purchase portions of shares for amounts as small as a few pounds. This chapter explores fractional shares not merely as a technical innovation but as a transformative doorway opening financial markets to millions who were previously excluded or hesitant. It articulates how fractional ownership operates, its implications for investor identity and behaviour, and the broader democratization of wealth-building.

At its core, fractional share investing breaks down the unitary nature of traditional stock ownership into divisible, micro units. Instead of purchasing a whole share priced at hundreds or even thousands of pounds, an investor can acquire, for example, 0.01 or 0.05 of a share. This fractional approach enables investing with remarkably low capital—sometimes as little as £5—while still granting proportional ownership benefits such as dividends and capital appreciation. Platforms like Robinhood, Fidelity, M1 Finance, and Trading 212 have pioneered this offering, leveraging sophisticated backend systems that aggregate, allocate, and reconcile fractional transactions efficiently. The mechanics involve pooling fractional orders from multiple investors, enabling market makers to transact whole shares and distributing fractional entitlements accordingly. Understanding this operational foundation dispels misconceptions about fractional shares being "not real" or somehow lesser forms of ownership.

Beyond the mechanics lies the profound psychological impact fractional shares have on investors, particularly those with limited resources. Ownership—no matter how small—instantiates a shift in self-concept from passive observer to active participant in the financial markets. This shift carries considerable behavioural consequences. Research in behavioural finance shows that even minimal stakes heighten engagement, encourage learning, and reduce psychological distance from investing. For instance, studies tracking user behaviour on fractional investing platforms indicate that investors with fractional shares exhibit higher contribution rates and more frequent portfolio reviews compared to those with traditional whole-share holdings. The act of owning a piece of a leading company—however tiny—imbues confidence and a sense of agency, catalysing a virtuous cycle of investment and education.

Real-world examples underscore the accessibility fractional shares provide. Consider a young professional, Emma, who begins investing with £10 a month in fractional shares of companies she admires. This modest investment allows her to build a diversified portfolio over time, previously unimaginable on her income level. Emma's experience contrasts sharply with the traditional narrative requiring lump-sum capital and high entry thresholds, illustrating how fractional shares expand inclusion. Similarly, retirees or low-income earners can participate meaningfully in equity markets, smoothing pathways to wealth accumulation and financial security.

However, fractional shares also introduce nuanced challenges and debates. One tension concerns liquidity and transferability: fractional shares are often custodied within proprietary platforms, limiting direct transfer or sale outside the ecosystem. While this is generally transparent and acceptable to many users, it raises questions about ownership rights and market control. Moreover, fractional trading may involve fees or bid-ask spreads that disproportionately affect micro-investors. The chapter addresses these considerations candidly, advising readers on how to evaluate platforms critically, understand cost structures, and protect their interests.

The democratization of investing through fractional shares intersects with broader financial innovations, such as micro-savings, robo-advisors, and automated investing. Fractional ownership is a foundational building block enabling these services to function at scale for low-income investors. By combining fractional shares with automated contributions, users can incrementally build portfolios without active decision-making, reducing behavioural barriers like procrastination and analysis paralysis. This synergy illustrates how fractional shares are not an isolated novelty but a catalyst for holistic, inclusive financial ecosystems.

Philosophically, fractional shares challenge entrenched notions of ownership and value. They invite reconsideration of what it means to "own" a company and participate in capital markets. Does owning a fraction of a share confer the same economic and psychological rights as whole ownership? How does this fractional model reshape collective shareholder power and corporate governance? The chapter engages these questions, weaving insights from legal scholarship, economics, and ethics to illuminate the complex implications of fragmented ownership.

Technology's role is paramount yet double-edged. On one hand, fintech platforms democratise access, streamline transactions, and personalise investing. On the other, they raise issues of platform dependence, data privacy, and digital literacy. Investors must navigate these dynamics thoughtfully, balancing convenience with vigilance. The chapter provides practical guidance on selecting trustworthy platforms, understanding terms of service, and maintaining autonomy in digital investing.

The cultural impact of fractional shares is significant. By enabling ownership for all income levels, fractional investing disrupts social narratives that equate market participation with wealth or status. It fosters a more egalitarian financial culture, where the act of investing is accessible, relatable, and empowering. This shift holds potential for reducing wealth inequality and reshaping financial education, making investing a lived experience rather than an abstract ideal.

This chapter, through detailed explanation, real-life examples, and critical analysis, positions fractional shares as a revolutionary doorway to investing. It equips readers to understand the mechanics, benefits, and challenges of fractional ownership, preparing them to engage confidently and thoughtfully in this new financial landscape. Far from a mere technical detail, fractional shares represent a profound expansion of who can own, participate, and build wealth—transforming investing from a distant privilege into a tangible, everyday opportunity.

The ETF is Your Friend: Demystifying Global Diversification

In the evolving landscape of personal finance, Exchange-Traded Funds or ETFs—have emerged as one of the most powerful, yet often misunderstood, tools available to individual investors. Once the exclusive realm of institutional players, ETFs have been propelled into mainstream accessibility by technological advances and regulatory reforms, transforming how people engage with financial markets. For many, the complexity and jargon surrounding ETFs can feel daunting, leading to hesitation or missed opportunities. This chapter seeks to strip away the layers of opacity, presenting ETFs in plain English while illuminating their unique capacity to unlock *global diversification*—a cornerstone of risk management and long-term wealth building. Far from esoteric instruments, ETFs can serve as trusted allies that enable even small investors to access broad, diversified portfolios with simplicity, efficiency, and affordability.

At their simplest, ETFs are investment funds traded on stock exchanges, much like individual shares. Unlike mutual funds, which are bought and sold directly through fund managers at the end of trading days, ETFs trade continuously throughout the day at market prices. This liquidity and flexibility give investors immediate access and transparency, allowing them to enter or exit positions with ease. Crucially, ETFs hold baskets of assets—ranging from stocks and bonds to commodities or real estate—aggregating diverse holdings into a single tradable security. This structure makes ETFs a highly efficient vehicle for diversification: with one purchase, an investor can gain exposure to dozens, hundreds, or even thousands of underlying securities, spreading risk across sectors, geographies, and asset classes.

Understanding the mechanics of ETFs dispels much of the mystique. Many ETFs track specific indices, such as the FTSE 100, the S&P 500, or the MSCI Emerging Markets Index. By mirroring the composition of these indices, ETFs provide a passive investment approach that tends to have lower costs compared to actively managed funds. The passive nature also sidesteps common pitfalls like manager bias or excessive trading. This means that when you invest in an ETF tracking the S&P 500, for example, you effectively own fractional shares of the 500 largest U.S. companies—Apple, Microsoft, Amazon, and beyond—without the need to buy each stock individually. This access broadens not only diversification but also market participation, allowing investors to benefit from the collective growth of an entire economy or sector.

Global diversification, a concept fundamental to modern portfolio theory, is made remarkably accessible through ETFs. Historically, investors faced significant hurdles to owning foreign assets, including high transaction costs, regulatory complexities, and currency risks. ETFs dismantle many of these barriers by pooling investments from across borders into a single instrument. Whether seeking exposure to developed markets like Japan and Germany or emerging economies in Asia, Africa, or Latin America, investors can select ETFs tailored to their geographic and sectoral preferences. This international reach dilutes concentration risk—the vulnerability of a portfolio overly dependent on one country's economic fortunes—and smooths returns over time. The chapter illustrates these benefits with real-world data, contrasting concentrated portfolios against diversified ETF holdings to underscore risk reduction and return stability.

The accessibility and affordability of ETFs are critical for investors with modest means. Many ETFs have low minimum investment thresholds and offer fractional trading, allowing investors to build diversified portfolios incrementally. Expense ratios—the annual fees charged by funds—tend to be among the lowest in the industry, preserving more of the investor's returns. Moreover, ETFs benefit from tax efficiencies; their structure generally results in fewer capital gains distributions compared to mutual funds, reducing tax drag on investments. These attributes align well with the needs of small and irregular investors, empowering them to participate in global markets without prohibitive costs or complexity.

Despite their advantages, ETFs are not without nuances and risks that warrant careful consideration. For instance, while most ETFs are passively managed, some employ active strategies or track niche sectors with greater volatility. Understanding the fund's objective, holdings, and risk profile is essential to avoid mismatches between expectations and reality. Additionally, currency fluctuations can impact returns on international ETFs, a factor often overlooked by novice investors. The chapter delves into these aspects, providing practical guidance on evaluating ETFs, interpreting prospectuses, and aligning investments with personal risk tolerance and goals.

The proliferation of ETFs has also sparked debates within the financial community. Critics argue that the sheer volume of available ETFs—numbering in the thousands—can overwhelm investors, leading to choice paralysis or suboptimal selections. Others caution that ETF popularity might inflate asset prices or reduce market efficiency. The chapter presents these perspectives alongside counterarguments, fostering a balanced understanding of the evolving ETF ecosystem. It encourages readers to approach ETFs with critical curiosity, informed judgement, and a long-term horizon.

Case studies feature prominently to ground theory in lived experience. For example, an early-career professional using a global equity ETF to complement her savings plan discovers how passive diversification buffers volatility and supports steady growth. A retiree relying on bond ETFs illustrates how fixed income exposure can provide income and capital preservation without the need for complex management. These narratives demonstrate how ETFs serve diverse investment objectives across life stages, reinforcing their versatility.

Technology's role in facilitating ETF investing cannot be overstated. Online brokerages, mobile apps, and robo-advisors have simplified access, research, and execution, putting global diversification within reach of anyone with a smartphone and internet connection. However, the chapter warns against complacency, urging investors to cultivate financial literacy and remain vigilant about fees, tax implications, and portfolio coherence.

Beyond the mechanics and strategies, this chapter situates ETFs within a broader philosophical and cultural shift toward inclusive, democratized investing. By enabling small-scale, diversified ownership, ETFs contribute to dismantling traditional hierarchies in wealth accumulation, challenging the notion that global markets are reserved for elites. This democratization fosters greater financial agency, resilience, and participation—values central to the book's overarching ethos.

Through clear explanation, empirical evidence, and thoughtful analysis, this chapter transforms the intimidating concept of ETFs into an accessible, actionable tool for readers. It equips investors to harness ETFs not as opaque financial products but as practical friends—trusted instruments that open doors to global diversification, risk management, and meaningful wealth-building. In doing so, it redefines what is possible for those starting small, turning complexity into clarity and exclusion into opportunity.

Crypto as High-Volatility Confidence Practice

Cryptocurrency remains one of the most polarising and misunderstood investment arenas of the contemporary financial landscape. Its reputation oscillates wildly—from revolutionary technology promising a decentralised financial future to speculative mania fraught with volatility and regulatory uncertainty. For the cautious or resource-limited investor, the question often arises: can crypto play a constructive role in personal finance, especially when investing modest sums? This chapter argues that, when approached thoughtfully, even a $10 investment in cryptocurrency can serve as a *high-volatility confidence practice*—a deliberate, small-scale exercise that cultivates financial literacy, emotional resilience, and technological fluency. This perspective reframes crypto not merely as an asset class but as a behavioural and educational tool, empowering investors to navigate complexity and uncertainty with greater courage and awareness.

The inherent volatility of cryptocurrencies like Bitcoin, Ethereum, and their numerous derivatives is well-documented and often portrayed as a disqualifying risk for everyday investors. Price swings of 10% or more in a single day are commonplace, starkly contrasting with the more measured movements of traditional equities or bonds. Yet, this very volatility creates a unique experiential laboratory where investors confront and learn to manage emotional responses—fear, greed, impatience, and optimism—in real time. The *psychology of high-volatility investing* offers critical insights into human decision-making under uncertainty. Engaging with crypto in small, manageable amounts allows investors to develop *emotional agility*—the capacity to observe reactions without being overwhelmed or driven to impulsive actions. This emotional training is invaluable, cultivating a mindset that can be applied across all investing spheres.

Empirical studies in behavioural finance show that experiential learning—actively participating in markets—enhances financial literacy far more effectively than passive reading or theoretical education alone. Crypto's accessibility, via user-friendly apps and low minimum entry points, invites new investors to engage practically with portfolio construction, digital wallets, transaction processes, and market timing considerations. For many, purchasing a small amount of cryptocurrency becomes a catalyst for exploring blockchain technology, decentralised finance (DeFi), and the broader digital economy. This hands-on exposure demystifies complex concepts, reducing technophobia and fostering digital confidence. Case studies illustrate individuals who began with minimal crypto investments and evolved into informed participants capable of evaluating emerging technologies critically.

However, the chapter does not advocate uncritical enthusiasm. It emphasises *intentionality* in crypto engagement, cautioning against viewing it as a get-rich-quick scheme or pure speculation. Distinguishing between gambling and investing is crucial, especially in high-volatility contexts. Investors must anchor their crypto activities within broader financial goals, risk tolerances, and time horizons. By framing small crypto investments as confidence-building exercises rather than wealth guarantees, the approach aligns with responsible money management principles. This mindset encourages disciplined investment habits, continual learning, and emotional balance.

Regulatory landscapes and security concerns present additional layers of complexity. The chapter navigates these issues, elucidating how differing national regulations impact access, taxation, and protections. It highlights best practices for safeguarding digital assets, including the use of hardware wallets, multi-factor authentication, and reputable exchanges. Understanding these safeguards enhances investor agency and mitigates risks of fraud or loss.

Ethical and environmental considerations also arise in the crypto domain. Energy consumption debates surrounding proof-of-work cryptocurrencies invite reflection on aligning investment choices with personal values. The chapter explores emerging trends such as proof-of-stake mechanisms and carbon-neutral initiatives, equipping readers to factor sustainability into their crypto decisions.

Technological innovation in crypto investing is rapid and evolving. The chapter surveys developments such as fractionalised NFTs, tokenised assets, and automated yield farming, clarifying which innovations hold potential for mainstream investors and which remain experimental. It underscores the importance of foundational understanding before venturing into complex instruments, ensuring investors maintain clarity amid novelty.

By engaging with crypto as a high-volatility confidence practice, investors develop *a suite of transferable skills*—from managing risk tolerance and emotional regulation to deepening digital literacy and financial autonomy. This experiential learning transcends crypto itself, enriching overall investment competence. The chapter advocates integrating crypto thoughtfully within diversified portfolios, complementing more stable asset classes rather than dominating them.

Through a blend of behavioural science, technology insight, and pragmatic guidance, this chapter reframes modest crypto investing as a purposeful, educational journey. It invites readers to approach crypto with curiosity tempered by caution, recognising that the true value lies not only in potential financial returns but in the *development of confidence, resilience, and understanding* essential for navigating the complex modern financial world.

Owning vs. Gambling: Recognising When Small Investments Build Long-Term Value or Feed Emotional Adrenaline

The allure of investing can sometimes blur into the thrill of gambling, especially when capital is scarce and stakes feel personal. For the small-scale investor, distinguishing between *owning*—a deliberate act of wealth-building—and *gambling*—a reactive pursuit of quick gains fueled by emotional highs—can be challenging but is essential for sustainable financial progress. This chapter equips readers with a nuanced understanding of these divergent mindsets and behaviours, offering conceptual clarity, practical tools, and reflective frameworks to discern when an investment aligns with long-term value creation versus when it merely feeds emotional adrenaline. By cultivating this discernment, investors can foster patience, reduce impulsivity, and ultimately make decisions that reinforce resilience and growth.

Ownership, at its core, is about *intentionality* and *time horizon.* It involves acquiring assets with a clear-eyed view toward long-term appreciation, income generation, or strategic portfolio diversification. Owning implies an acceptance of market volatility and a commitment to weather fluctuations with composure, grounded in research and alignment with personal financial goals. In contrast, gambling is characterised by *speculation* driven by immediate gratification, fear of missing out, or the lure of rapid returns. Gambling often involves high-risk, short-term bets with disproportionate exposure relative to one's capital or understanding, frequently accompanied by emotional rollercoasters—excitement, anxiety, regret—that undermine rational decision-making.

Behavioural finance provides a robust lens through which to examine this dichotomy. Research indicates that emotional arousal—triggered by rapid price movements, social media hype, or anecdotal "success stories"—can hijack cognitive control, leading to impulsive trades, overtrading, and suboptimal outcomes. The dopamine-driven reward circuitry in the brain responds to the suspense and thrill of high-stakes betting, reinforcing patterns that resemble gambling more than prudent investing. Understanding these neuropsychological underpinnings arms investors with awareness to recognise when they are acting from impulse rather than informed strategy.

A critical marker of ownership versus gambling lies in *due diligence and knowledge*. Ownership entails engagement with fundamental analysis, valuation metrics, and economic context. Investors who own their assets understand the underlying business models, revenue streams, competitive advantages, and macroeconomic drivers. Gambling, by contrast, often relies on tip-driven decisions, trend-chasing, or hearsay without substantive evaluation. The chapter provides frameworks for conducting accessible due diligence tailored to small investors, emphasising the importance of education as a bulwark against impulsivity.

Risk management further distinguishes owning from gambling. Owners typically allocate only a manageable portion of their capital to high-risk positions and maintain diversified portfolios to mitigate potential losses. Gamblers may concentrate resources on volatile assets without safeguards, exposing themselves to ruinous drawdowns. The chapter introduces pragmatic risk assessment tools and portfolio construction principles designed for micro-investors, illustrating how measured exposure supports endurance through market cycles.

The temporal dimension is equally instructive. Ownership embraces *time as an ally*, recognising that compound growth and recovery from downturns require patience. Gambling fixates on immediate outcomes, often abandoning positions prematurely or doubling down recklessly. Case studies demonstrate how investors who maintain disciplined time horizons outperform those swayed by short-term noise, reinforcing the virtue of persistence.

Emotional self-regulation is paramount. The chapter offers techniques grounded in mindfulness and cognitive behavioural therapy to identify and manage emotional triggers that prompt gambling behaviour. By cultivating emotional literacy, investors gain the capacity to pause, reflect, and recalibrate decisions rather than react reflexively to market stimuli.

Technology's dual role is explored with nuance. While trading apps and social platforms democratise access, their design often prioritises engagement over deliberation, sometimes fostering gambling-like behaviours. The chapter advises on mindful use of technology—setting limits, disabling impulsive notifications, and focusing on goal-oriented platforms—to support ownership mindsets.

Ethical reflection deepens the discourse. The glamorisation of speculative "get rich quick" narratives can perpetuate harmful societal myths equating financial worth with risk-taking bravado. This chapter challenges such norms, advocating for dignity, patience, and sustainable growth as hallmarks of true financial empowerment.

Ownership and gambling also diverge in community impact. Owners contribute to capital formation, supporting businesses and economic development. Gamblers, while sometimes providing market liquidity, may amplify volatility and encourage herd behaviour detrimental to market stability. Recognising this distinction fosters a broader sense of responsibility and alignment with values beyond personal gain.

Through richly detailed examples, including profiles of investors who transformed impulsive tendencies into disciplined ownership and those who succumbed to gambling pitfalls, readers gain practical insight and motivation. These narratives reveal that the transition from gambling to owning is not merely behavioural but deeply psychological, requiring commitment, education, and self-compassion.

Ultimately, this chapter reframes small-scale investing as a practice of *intentional ownership*—one that privileges strategic vision over fleeting excitement, education over hearsay, and resilience over reaction. It empowers readers to recognise their agency, make informed choices, and cultivate a financial identity rooted in long-term value creation rather than ephemeral thrills. This discernment is foundational to converting modest capital into enduring wealth and transforming the investor from a transient participant into a steady architect of their financial future.

Chapter 7
Automate or Forget—Systems that Keep Investing Alive

The adage "default is destiny" captures a central truth in behavioural finance: left to their own devices, humans will follow the path of least resistance, and this inertia often shapes long-term outcomes. For investors with modest incomes—juggling irregular schedules, tight budgets, and limited mental bandwidth—this is not abstract theory but daily reality. Consistent investing, widely recognised as crucial to wealth-building, can easily fall victim to competing pressures, fatigue, or simple forgetfulness. The solution, as this chapter reveals, is less about heroically exercising willpower and more about designing systems that automate investment behaviour, turning sporadic intentions into sustained momentum. The mantra "automate or forget" is deceptively simple yet profoundly effective: by constructing financial ecosystems that operate on autopilot, investors free cognitive space while ensuring their money works quietly, reliably, and continuously.

Automation is no longer a privilege reserved for institutional players or the wealthy. Today, digital tools—from payroll deductions to mobile apps with round-up features, robo-advisors, and direct deposit allocations—put autopilot investing within reach of virtually anyone. Yet availability alone does not guarantee success. This chapter explores how to establish automation systems that align with the realities of low-income earners: fluctuating cash flows, unpredictable pay schedules, and the psychological barriers of committing small, regular amounts. It goes beyond generic advice, illustrating how default mechanisms can be customised and optimised to bridge the gap between intention and execution.

The opening section, *Default is Destiny*, unpacks the behavioural science underpinning automatic investing. Human decision-making is effortful; repeated choices deplete self-control and increase the likelihood of procrastination or abandonment. By embedding contributions into existing routines—payroll deductions, app-based round-ups tied to everyday transactions—investors sidestep the inconsistencies of manual effort. Practical guidance details setup options that minimise disruption while maximising regularity and compounding potential. Real-world examples show how seemingly trivial automated micro-investments grow into meaningful portfolios over time.

Moving from theory to practice, the chapter addresses *Use the App, Not Just the Idea*. Technology, though empowering, can overwhelm or mislead low-income users if applied carelessly. The chapter evaluates popular platforms—Acorns, Fidelity Spire, Cash App, Stash—on usability, fees, educational support, and integration with other tools. It emphasises minimalist, low-cost, user-centric solutions, highlighting app features such as round-ups, recurring transfers, and goal tracking, which translate abstract ambitions into tangible progress.

Yet automation is not abdication. The section *Fire-and-Forget Doesn't Mean Check-Out* challenges the notion that autopilot absolves active engagement. Instead, it promotes structured "Wealth Check-Ins"—quarterly or biannual reviews to assess portfolio performance, rebalance allocations, and recalibrate goals. This approach balances cognitive efficiency with intentional oversight, preventing drift or complacency without falling into analysis paralysis. Templates and reflective prompts equip readers to conduct these reviews confidently, transforming what might seem intimidating into an empowering ritual.

Perhaps the most profound insight emerges in *Letting Technology Be Your Willpower*. Willpower is finite, especially for those navigating economic uncertainty, precarious work, or caregiving responsibilities. Automation acts as an external discipline, an architectural design that substitutes for depleted self-control. By reducing friction—delays, forgetfulness, temptation—investors create environments that nudge behaviour toward positive financial habits without heroic effort. Concepts from behavioural economics and design thinking demonstrate how intentional defaults, timely reminders, and seamless integration can sustain investing behaviours amid life's unpredictability.

The chapter also acknowledges pitfalls and ethical considerations. Over-reliance on automation without understanding fundamentals is risky; readers are urged to complement technology with financial literacy. Transparency regarding fees and data privacy is critical, as is maintaining agency within automated systems. Systemic barriers—such as limited access to payroll or app-based tools—are addressed, with guidance on alternatives and advocacy for inclusivity.

Illustrative case studies bring these principles to life. Low-income earners navigating irregular pay cycles and competing expenses—through round-up apps, small payroll deductions, or scheduled transfers—demonstrate how automated micro-actions generate momentum that compounds beyond financial returns, fostering optimism, agency, and control.

Philosophically, the chapter situates automation within a broader reconception of financial agency. Discipline is reframed not solely as an internal virtue but as the product of intentional environment design. Automation is neither a crutch nor a substitute for engagement; it is a strategic partnership between human intention and technological facilitation—a synergy essential for sustained wealth-building in modern, complex realities.

In sum, this chapter presents a comprehensive, evidence-based roadmap for embedding automation as a cornerstone of everyday investing. It guides readers from sporadic enthusiasm toward resilient, self-sustaining systems, ensuring their financial goals advance with minimal cognitive load. By embracing "automate or forget," investors convert the chaos of daily life into a steady engine for wealth accumulation, cultivating consistent momentum that quietly shapes their financial future.

Default is Destiny: Setting Up Autopilot Investing for Lasting Momentum

In the landscape of personal finance, the maxim "default is destiny" resonates with unyielding force. The human tendency to adhere to pre-set options—the path of least resistance—shapes not only daily habits but also long-term financial outcomes. For those managing limited incomes or variable cash flows, this behavioural insight is a gateway to empowerment. The simple act of setting up *autopilot investing* transforms intention into consistent practice, bypassing the often insurmountable barriers of willpower, distraction, and decision fatigue. This subchapter explores the mechanics, psychology, and practicalities of embedding investing into automated systems—payroll deductions, app integrations, and round-up features—that operate quietly in the background, ensuring that wealth-building becomes not a sporadic event but a seamless, ongoing process.

The psychology behind default options is well-established in behavioural economics. Studies demonstrate that individuals overwhelmingly accept default settings, whether it be organ donation consent or retirement plan enrolment, due to cognitive ease and perceived endorsement. When investing is wired as a default behaviour—an automatic deduction from wages or a small, recurring transfer to a brokerage account—the inertia that typically undermines financial consistency becomes a powerful ally. Rather than requiring active decisions each month, the investment contribution is embedded in the fabric of routine, enabling the investor to sidestep the self-sabotage of procrastination or hesitation.

Among the most effective mechanisms for autopilot investing is *payroll deduction*. This method, long utilised in employer-sponsored retirement plans, allows a fixed amount or percentage of earnings to be directed straight from salary to investment accounts before the money even touches the individual's hands. For employees with access to such schemes, payroll deduction leverages structural discipline and removes temptation. However, the concept is equally adaptable for those outside traditional employment frameworks. Freelancers and gig workers can set up scheduled transfers aligned with expected payment cycles, effectively mimicking the payroll model. The challenge lies in creating systems flexible enough to accommodate income variability, a task addressed later in the chapter but central to this discussion.

Technological innovation has vastly expanded the toolkit for autopilot investing. *App integrations* represent a frontier where convenience meets behavioural science. Platforms like Acorns,

Stash, and Robinhood offer features that connect directly to bank accounts, automating investments with minimal user intervention. These apps often include round-up systems, wherein everyday purchases are rounded up to the nearest dollar and the spare change allocated to an investment portfolio. Such micro-investments harness the cumulative power of small amounts, making investing feel accessible and low-risk. Importantly, these systems democratise participation, allowing individuals with modest means to engage without large upfront commitments or technical expertise.

Round-up systems deserve special attention for their dual function: they simplify the financial commitment and transform the act of spending into an opportunity for saving and investing. For example, a coffee purchase for £2.75 becomes an £3.00 transaction, with 25p diverted to investments. Over time, these seemingly trivial amounts aggregate into meaningful capital. Beyond financial accumulation, round-ups cultivate a *mindset shift*—viewing money as a continuous flow with an investment component rather than a finite resource to be exhausted. This reframing supports emotional resilience and encourages consistent engagement.

Despite the evident advantages of automation, the transition to autopilot investing is not without complexities. One salient tension arises from *trust and control*. Entrusting technology or third-party systems with financial flows can evoke anxiety, particularly among those historically marginalised by financial institutions. Transparency and user education are critical to overcoming such barriers. The chapter recommends strategies for verifying app security, understanding fee structures, and maintaining oversight through periodic account reviews. Far from relinquishing control, automation when combined with informed vigilance constitutes a *partnership* between investor and technology, balancing convenience with accountability.

Another challenge is the design of automation that respects the realities of low-income and variable-income earners. Fixed deductions may prove untenable when paychecks fluctuate or unexpected expenses arise. Adaptive systems that allow flexible contribution levels, pausing mechanisms, or percentage-based deductions can accommodate such volatility without penalising the investor. This adaptability transforms automation from a rigid rule into a *responsive tool*, supporting sustained investing even amid financial instability.

Case studies illuminate the transformative impact of autopilot investing. For instance, an individual earning £1,200 monthly with irregular freelance income set up a percentage-based automated transfer to a low-cost index fund. Over eighteen months, this practice generated a modest but growing portfolio, while the investor reported increased confidence and decreased financial stress. Another example details a retail worker who linked round-up technology to her debit card, accumulating over £300 in investments within a year without altering spending habits significantly. These narratives underscore that automation empowers investors to transcend the limitations of time, attention, and fluctuating motivation.

Ethically, embedding investing as a default aligns with broader goals of financial inclusion and equity. Automation reduces barriers to entry, mitigates cognitive overload, and encourages disciplined behaviour—factors often unavailable to low-income groups. However, caution is warranted to ensure that automated products do not exploit vulnerability through excessive fees, opaque terms, or predatory marketing. The chapter advocates for regulatory oversight and consumer education as complementary forces to technological innovation.

Philosophically, the principle of "default is destiny" challenges cultural notions that financial discipline is solely an individual moral virtue. Instead, it highlights the power of *environmental design* and structural supports in shaping behaviour. This shift democratizes responsibility, urging institutions, employers, and technology developers to create frameworks that enable positive defaults for all economic strata. For individuals, it reframes investing not as an intermittent struggle of will but as a cultivated habit embedded in daily life.

In summary, setting up autopilot investing via payroll deductions, app integrations, or round-up systems represents a practical and psychologically sound strategy for transforming sporadic saving into continuous wealth-building. By harnessing the power of defaults, investors can create resilient financial practices that endure beyond fluctuating motivation and external distractions. This approach offers a scalable, inclusive pathway to investing that honours the realities of small incomes while opening doors to the long-term benefits of compound growth and financial agency.

Use the App, Not Just the Idea: Evaluating Investment Tools for Low-Income Users

In the digital age, the promise of investing has become increasingly accessible. Yet, for many low-income earners, the gap between *knowing* that investing is crucial and *actually doing* it remains wide. The proliferation of investment apps and platforms has generated a surge of interest and opportunity, but the challenge is not merely to have an investing app installed—it is to engage with tools that truly accommodate the unique constraints, rhythms, and aspirations of those with limited financial resources. This section delves deeply into the practical realities of using investment apps in the context of low-income users, examining which platforms deliver meaningful value, how they align with users' needs, and what pitfalls to avoid. The goal is to transform the abstract appeal of investing into concrete, manageable action by guiding readers to *use the app*—not just embrace the idea.

Investment apps have democratized entry, lowering traditional barriers like high minimum deposits and complex procedures. However, accessibility is multifaceted; it extends beyond mere availability to encompass affordability, usability, transparency, and relevance to the user's financial context. Many low-income earners face fluctuating incomes, precarious employment, and competing financial demands that call for tools designed with flexibility and simplicity at their core. Without this thoughtful alignment, apps risk becoming another source of frustration, disillusionment, or even financial harm.

Among the most prominent platforms serving low-to-moderate income investors are Acorns, Fidelity Spire, Cash App Investing, and Stash. Each offers distinctive features and fee structures that warrant detailed consideration. Acorns, for example, has popularized the "round-up" model, where purchases are rounded up to the nearest dollar, and spare change is automatically invested. This micro-investing approach leverages behavioural psychology by making investment contributions seamless and incremental. For users with small, irregular cash flows, this can be a powerful mechanism to build wealth without conscious budgeting shifts. However, Acorns charges a monthly fee that can be significant relative to tiny account balances, raising concerns about fee-to-value ratios. This tension illustrates a broader challenge: *balancing cost structures with service benefits* to avoid eroding the very capital users seek to grow.

Fidelity Spire distinguishes itself by integrating goal-setting and financial planning tools with investing, presenting a holistic approach rather than isolated transactions. For low-income users, who often juggle multiple competing goals—from emergency savings to debt repayment—this comprehensive design can facilitate prioritization and progress tracking. Yet, its effectiveness hinges on user engagement and financial literacy; the platform demands a degree of discipline and initiative that some beginners may find daunting. This points to the crucial role of *educational support and intuitive design* in app success.

Cash App Investing appeals through simplicity and zero-commission trades, allowing fractional share purchases starting at $1. Its social features, such as sharing investment activity with contacts, create communal reinforcement, which can motivate sustained participation. However, the gamified interface may blur lines between investing and speculation, risking impulsive behaviour among vulnerable users. This raises ethical questions about *the responsibility of app developers* in designing user interfaces that foster prudent habits rather than addictive patterns.

Stash positions itself as an educational platform, combining low minimum investments with curated portfolios and personalised advice. For low-income users seeking guided entry points, this blend of automation and human-centred content can mitigate overwhelm. Yet, like Acorns, Stash's subscription fees pose trade-offs that require careful evaluation relative to investment size. This highlights the importance of *transparent communication* about costs and benefits to empower informed choice.

A critical criterion transcending platform features is *ease of use*. For individuals balancing work, family, and financial stress, time is scarce and cognitive load high. Apps that minimise setup complexity, automate routine tasks, and provide clear, jargon-free interfaces enhance the likelihood of sustained engagement. Conversely, convoluted navigation, frequent alerts, or obscure terminology risk alienation and abandonment. User experience research confirms that *frictionless design is not a luxury but a necessity* for effective financial technology in low-income contexts.

Security and privacy considerations are equally paramount. Low-income users often represent targets for predatory practices and scams. Trust in an app's safeguarding of personal data and funds underpins willingness to commit scarce resources. Therefore, assessing platforms' regulatory compliance, encryption standards, and customer support responsiveness is indispensable. Readers are encouraged to prioritise apps with verifiable reputations and transparent policies, recognising that *trustworthiness is foundational to financial empowerment.*

Beyond the individual platform level, systemic issues affect app efficacy. For instance, not all employers facilitate payroll deductions that integrate with investment apps, limiting the automation potential for many low-income workers. Additionally, banking access disparities can restrict app usability. Recognising these structural constraints, the chapter advocates for complementary strategies—such as combining app use with community financial education, advocacy for inclusive banking services, and leveraging public programs—that collectively advance investing accessibility.

Importantly, this discussion situates app usage within the broader behavioural context. Investing is a habit cultivated over time, and apps function best as *tools within an ecosystem* that includes goal clarity, emotional regulation, and incremental learning. Overemphasis on technology alone risks overlooking the human factors that drive sustained financial behaviour. The chapter therefore underscores the value of pairing app engagement with reflective practices—journaling progress, celebrating small wins, and contextualising setbacks—to deepen commitment.

Real-world case studies enrich the analysis. For example, a young mother working multiple part-time jobs used a combination of Acorns' round-ups and Stash's educational modules to gradually build an investment portfolio despite income volatility. Another case follows a university student who leveraged Cash App's fractional shares to experiment with stock ownership, gaining confidence that translated into more deliberate, diversified investing. These narratives demonstrate that while no app is a panacea, thoughtful selection and consistent use can catalyse transformative financial journeys.

In sum, *using the app—not just embracing the idea*—requires intentionality, critical evaluation, and alignment with personal circumstances. The promise of technology is real, but its power unfolds only when harnessed with discernment and supported by contextual understanding. This subchapter equips readers with the insights and frameworks to navigate the complex landscape of investment apps, empowering them to transform digital possibilities into tangible progress on their wealth-building paths.

Fire-and-Forget Doesn't Mean Check-Out: Navigating Periodic Investment Reviews with Clarity and Confidence

The allure of autopilot investing is undeniable. Setting up automated contributions, linking bank accounts to investment platforms, and enabling round-up features promise a hands-off approach to wealth-building that fits seamlessly into busy lives. Yet, the phrase "fire-and-forget" can dangerously mislead. It implies a once-and-done action, suggesting that after initiating an automated system, investors can fully disengage. Such disengagement, however, risks complacency, missed opportunities, or even the unintentional perpetuation of suboptimal choices. This paradox—that automation requires ongoing, but measured, attention—defines a critical frontier in personal investing. This article unpacks how investors, especially those with limited time or financial literacy, can embrace periodic reviews of their automated systems *without overthinking* or succumbing to decision fatigue. Striking this balance transforms automation from a passive crutch into an active partnership with one's financial future.

At the core lies the insight that *automation substitutes for willpower, not wisdom.* The mechanics of investing—transferring money, selecting funds, timing contributions—can be efficiently handled by technology. However, strategic choices about portfolio composition, risk tolerance, and changing life circumstances remain uniquely human decisions. Blind reliance on autopilot tools risks ossifying outdated allocations or ignoring shifts in personal goals. For example, an investor who set up a robo-advisor three years ago with a growth-oriented portfolio may find that their financial priorities have shifted towards capital preservation or homeownership, yet their automated contributions continue unchecked. Regular reviews serve as the corrective lens, recalibrating automated strategies to evolving realities.

The tension arises in how to conduct these reviews without descending into paralysis by analysis. For many low-income investors, time and cognitive bandwidth are scarce, and the emotional toll of financial decision-making can be high. Overthinking investment reviews can manifest as perfectionism, procrastination, or anxiety, undermining the very consistency automation aims to secure. Therefore, the concept of a *light-touch, scheduled review* emerges as an effective solution. For instance, setting quarterly or biannual calendar reminders to examine portfolio summaries, recent contributions, and performance metrics—without delving into minute daily fluctuations—enables meaningful oversight without overwhelm. This approach honours *emotional flexibility* alongside intellectual rigor.

The design of review processes benefits from simplicity and structure. Establishing a checklist that focuses on key questions—Are my goals still the same? Has my income or expense profile changed? Is my portfolio diversified appropriately? Have fees or app features evolved?—can channel attention to critical areas. Moreover, reframing reviews as *celebrations of progress* rather than audits of failure shifts the emotional tone, encouraging curiosity and resilience. Small wins, such as noticing steady growth or consistent contributions, build investor confidence, while recognizing and adjusting misalignments fosters proactive agency.

Real-world applications illustrate these principles. Take the example of Maria, a single parent working gig jobs with variable income. She automated a modest monthly transfer to an index fund, but initially hesitated to review her investments fearing complexity. Guided by a simple quarterly review plan, she now glances at her portfolio performance and reaffirms her commitment. When she experienced income fluctuations, she adjusted her transfer amounts accordingly, maintaining balance between investing and essential expenses. Maria's experience demonstrates that *periodic review need not be exhaustive to be effective*—rather, it serves as a dynamic check-in reinforcing sustainable practice.

Technological tools themselves can facilitate review without cognitive overload. Many investment platforms now include user-friendly dashboards, visual performance summaries, and educational nudges that prompt thoughtful reflection at appropriate intervals. For low-income investors, such tools lower barriers to engagement by translating complex data into intuitive insights. Yet, a caution remains: not all platforms encourage balanced review. Some may push frequent notifications or promote impulsive trades, which conflict with measured oversight. Users must therefore critically select apps that support *mindful interaction*, integrating automation with periodic, purposeful attention.

Ethical dimensions emerge around the notion of disengagement. While automation empowers, it can also create false security, particularly among vulnerable populations who may assume that "set it and forget it" absolves ongoing responsibility. Financial educators and advisors have a role in cultivating a mindset that values *responsible stewardship* over passive delegation. Encouraging clients to view automated investing as a living system—one requiring occasional tuning—shifts perceptions from relinquishing control to exercising thoughtful guardianship. This reframing combats disempowerment and enhances long-term financial wellbeing.

The dynamics of "fire-and-forget" also intersect with behavioural finance. Humans are prone to *recency bias* and emotional decision-making, which can lead to overreaction to market volatility or neglect of gradual portfolio drift. Automated systems buffer against impulsivity but periodic review helps counteract complacency. By stepping back at scheduled intervals, investors gain perspective, contextualising short-term noise within long-term objectives. This rhythm fosters *emotional resilience*, preventing burnout and sustaining commitment over decades.

It is essential to acknowledge that periodic review does not demand mastery of financial jargon or complex analytics. The emphasis is on *reflective engagement* rather than technical precision. For many, this might mean asking simple, honest questions about comfort with current investments or seeking trusted advice when uncertainties arise. The chapter therefore advocates cultivating a *culture of curiosity*, where learning and adaptation are continuous but manageable, supported by accessible resources and community networks.

In sum, the art of integrating automation with thoughtful review is a cornerstone of effective, enduring investing—especially for those navigating the constraints of small incomes and busy lives. Embracing that "fire-and-forget" is a misnomer frees investors to approach their portfolios as evolving systems requiring intermittent care. By adopting structured, low-burden review routines, leveraging supportive technology, and fostering adaptive mindsets, investors can unlock the full potential of automated investing. This balance between ease and engagement transforms passive default into active destiny, empowering readers to build wealth with both confidence and compassion.

Letting Technology Be Your Willpower:

In the realm of personal finance, willpower is often touted as the linchpin of successful investing and saving habits. Yet, the reality for many—especially those managing modest or fluctuating incomes—is that sheer willpower alone is neither reliable nor sustainable. Herein lies the transformative potential of technology, not as a mere convenience but as an *external discipline*—a scaffold that compensates for human frailty and environmental distractions. Automation emerges as a powerful ally, capable of embedding financial behaviours into the fabric of daily life, enabling consistency and resilience that outstrips raw self-control. This article explores how embracing technology as a surrogate for willpower reshapes the landscape of investing, particularly for those navigating the complexities of small income streams, unpredictable cash flow, and competing demands on time and attention.

Willpower, at its core, is a finite resource. Psychological research underscores that exerting self-control depletes cognitive energy, leaving individuals vulnerable to impulsive decisions once this reserve wanes. Financial decisions are especially prone to this dynamic, as they often compete with immediate emotional impulses, pressing expenses, and pervasive societal pressures to consume. Thus, relying exclusively on willpower to invest consistently can be a setup for failure. Here, technology's role transcends automation of transactions—it becomes an externalised form of self-regulation that operates independently of fluctuating motivation or stress levels. By delegating routine actions such as transferring funds, rebalancing portfolios, or making regular micro-investments to well-designed platforms, individuals reduce the cognitive load and sidestep common behavioural pitfalls.

This external discipline mirrors the concept of *choice architecture* in behavioural economics, where environments are structured to 'nudge' individuals toward beneficial behaviours. Apps that automatically round up purchases to invest spare change, or payroll deductions that funnel income directly into investment accounts, remove the need for frequent, deliberate decisions. Such features create an ecosystem in which good financial habits are the default path, rather than the exception requiring extraordinary effort. Importantly, this default setting aligns with what behavioural scientist BJ Fogg describes as "tiny habits"—small, easy-to-execute behaviours that, when consistently practiced, compound into meaningful change. Automation, therefore, is not a passive crutch but an active design choice that makes the desirable behaviour effortless and repeatable.

However, this paradigm invites critical scrutiny. Automation risks engendering complacency or disconnection from one's financial journey. For example, an investor might activate automated contributions but fail to engage with the underlying strategy, allowing portfolio drift or misaligned risk tolerance to persist unnoticed. Herein lies the imperative to view technology as *partner* rather than replacement for mindful stewardship. The best systems blend automation with periodic, low-effort reflection—empowering users to remain connected without overwhelming them. Such balance preserves agency while maximising consistency, striking a synergy between external discipline and internal oversight.

For low-income investors, this approach is particularly potent. Time and mental bandwidth are scarce commodities, and the emotional cost of financial management can be high. Automation not only reduces friction but also mitigates anxiety by transforming investing from a daunting, irregular chore into a seamless background process. Consider the psychological impact of a regular debit—knowing that a small amount is invested reliably, regardless of the day's stresses or distractions. This sense of steady progress, supported by technology, can reinforce identity as an investor and cultivate long-term commitment, even amid financial precarity.

Yet, the effectiveness of technological willpower hinges on thoughtful implementation. Not all apps or systems are created equal. Some may feature complex user interfaces, hidden fees, or incentives misaligned with the user's best interests. Furthermore, the proliferation of 'gamified' investing platforms, with their notifications and flashy dashboards, can inadvertently encourage impulsive behaviours rather than disciplined saving. Selecting tools that prioritise transparency, user control, and educational support is therefore critical. Trusted platforms that emphasise automation without overwhelming users enable the 'external discipline' function to flourish authentically.

Empirical studies lend weight to these observations. Research on automated savings programs reveals that participants are significantly more likely to accumulate emergency funds and maintain investment contributions than those relying on manual processes. These findings validate the premise that *environmental design and technological facilitation can triumph over the limitations of individual willpower*. Moreover, automation fosters emotional stability by minimizing decision fatigue and reducing exposure to the volatility of financial markets. By stabilising behavioural patterns, technology helps investors resist reactive behaviours that erode long-term wealth.

Ethically, positioning automation as willpower's proxy invites reflection on personal responsibility and empowerment. There is a delicate balance between utilising technology to support good habits and ceding too much control, risking detachment or passivity. Educators and advisors must frame automation not as abdication but as strategic delegation, a tool that amplifies human intention rather than replaces it. This perspective cultivates financial self-efficacy, encouraging users to engage periodically with their portfolios while trusting automation to maintain foundational consistency.

In practice, users can leverage a variety of automated mechanisms: payroll deductions that funnel a portion of earnings into investment accounts, recurring transfers scheduled immediately after income receipt to 'pay oneself first', app-based micro-investing services that round up daily spending, and robo-advisors that rebalance portfolios with minimal input. Each mechanism externalises specific facets of willpower, collectively constructing a robust support system that endures beyond fluctuating motivation.

Ultimately, letting technology serve as your willpower is about *designing a financial environment that enables you to succeed despite your human limitations*. It is a recognition that discipline is less about heroic self-control and more about smart systems that shape behaviour effortlessly. For investors operating within the constraints of small or unpredictable incomes, this approach offers a sustainable path to build wealth steadily and with less stress. Automation, when embraced thoughtfully, becomes the scaffolding upon which consistent, confident investing is built—transforming intention into action and aspiration into accumulation.

Chapter 8
Compound Interest is Quiet, but So Are Revolutions

In personal finance, compound interest is often hailed as the cornerstone of wealth-building—a seemingly magical mechanism by which modest, regular contributions grow into significant sums over time. Yet despite its frequent appearance in financial advice, its true potential is frequently misunderstood or undervalued, particularly by those starting with limited resources or later in life. This chapter urges readers to regard compounding not merely as a mathematical principle but as a transformative force capable of reshaping financial trajectories through patience and deliberate consistency. It challenges entrenched beliefs that small beginnings or delayed starts are futile, emphasising instead that time, persistence, and psychological engagement are among the most potent equalisers in investing.

At first glance, the mathematics of compound interest is straightforward: reinvested returns generate additional earnings, producing exponential growth. But the experiential reality of compounding—its cumulative power—rarely becomes apparent until years, often decades, of steady contributions and reinvestment bear visible fruit. Real-life illustrations show how even a few pounds set aside weekly can, over time, evolve into a substantial nest egg. These examples translate abstract formulas into lived experience, demonstrating how disciplined consistency outweighs the size of initial capital. Compound interest thus becomes more than arithmetic; it emerges as a narrative of patient accumulation, affirming that starting wherever one is—however small or late—is far from pointless.

Beyond numerical comprehension, the chapter underscores the value of visualisation in cultivating belief in compounding. Spreadsheets and growth charts have their place, yet interactive timelines, animated projections, and progress trackers engage the imagination in ways raw numbers cannot. This psychological layer is vital: investing relies as much on mindset as on mechanics.

Visualisation renders the abstract promise of compounding tangible, motivating, and emotionally resonant, helping investors maintain commitment through market volatility and personal financial fluctuations.

The chapter also confronts a common misconception: that beginning late or with limited funds dooms an investor to failure. Time, it argues, is not a rigid deadline but a flexible ally. By exploring the interplay of return rates, contribution amounts, and investment horizons, the narrative demonstrates how thoughtful adjustments and persistent effort can still produce meaningful growth. This perspective dismantles fatalistic thinking, shifting focus from immediate wealth accumulation toward cultivating a resilient financial identity reinforced by incremental progress.

Equally compelling is the exploration of emotional milestones—the moments when the abstract potential of compounding crystallises into tangible satisfaction. These are not merely numerical achievements but psychological affirmations, where patience is rewarded with pride and perseverance validated. Anecdotes from investors with modest or irregular incomes highlight how recognising and celebrating such milestones strengthens motivation and deepens the commitment to long-term investing. Here, compound interest transcends dry calculation to become a lived, identity-affirming practice.

By weaving together the mathematical, visual, temporal, and emotional dimensions of compounding, this chapter presents a comprehensive framework for understanding and harnessing one of investing's most powerful forces. It offers readers not only technical insight but also perspective and inspiration—encouraging them to embrace compound interest as a quiet revolution. With deliberate patience and consistent effort, small, regular actions accumulate into enduring wealth, cultivating both financial security and a sense of agency that extends far beyond mere numbers.

The Math of Patience:

The power of patience in investing is a lesson often overshadowed by the allure of quick returns and instant gratification. Yet, it is precisely this quality—patience—that transforms modest, consistent investments into substantial wealth over time. The mathematics of compound interest may appear straightforward, but its profound implications are best understood through vivid, real-world examples that demonstrate how even tiny contributions, when maintained steadily over decades, can lead to remarkable financial outcomes. This subchapter aims to illuminate the fundamental truth that in investing, *time is not the enemy but the greatest ally*, and that the discipline of small, patient steps is the foundation upon which lasting financial security is built.

Consider, for example, the story of Jane, a young professional who began investing just £5 per week at age 25. Over the span of forty years, without increasing her weekly contribution, Jane's disciplined savings, compounded annually at a modest average return of 7%, grew to approximately £35,000. This sum, while modest compared to the headlines of overnight millionaires, represents a meaningful nest egg assembled with minimal financial strain—a testament to the exponential growth power embedded in compound interest. Jane's experience is emblematic of a broader principle: *consistent small investments, left to mature over time, often outpace larger, erratic contributions made sporadically*. It is the regularity and patience, not the magnitude of individual contributions, that sets the stage for growth.

Delving deeper, the mathematics of patience is captured by the formula for compound interest:
$FV = PV \times (1 + r)^n$,
where FV is the future value, PV the present value or initial investment, r the annual return rate, and n the number of years invested. While this formula is deceptively simple, its consequences are profound. For instance, an initial investment of £1,000 compounded annually at 7% grows to nearly £15,000 after 40 years. However, by adding just £5 weekly—a mere £260 annually—Jane effectively augmented this growth trajectory, underscoring that *small incremental inputs can dramatically alter the compound outcome*. This amplification through steady additions is the

practical backbone of long-term wealth building for those with limited income.

Yet, the emotional and psychological dimensions of embracing patience in investing deserve equal attention. The gradual nature of compounding can challenge even the most committed investor. In a culture fixated on immediacy, waiting decades to see tangible results can test resolve. However, research in behavioural finance reveals that visualising growth through charts and progress trackers can mitigate impatience, fostering a sense of accomplishment and reinforcing commitment. For example, digital tools that project future values of current investments provide a tangible representation of compounding, translating abstract percentages into relatable narratives of potential achievement. This interplay of math and mindset is crucial: understanding the numbers intellectually is one step; internalising their significance emotionally is another.

Contrasting perspectives emerge when considering those who delay investing, convinced that starting late renders compounding ineffective. While it is true that early investment maximises growth potential, it is a misconception to deem late starters doomed. Consider Michael, who began investing £50 monthly at age 45 with the same 7% return. By retirement at 65, he accumulated over £28,000—a substantial sum reflecting that *time remains a powerful factor, even when the investment horizon shortens*. Michael's case highlights the adaptive potential within compounding math: increased contributions and disciplined saving, even over two decades, can yield meaningful results. This reframing dispels fatalistic attitudes and invites actionable optimism.

Furthermore, the subtlety of compounding extends to the choice of investment vehicles. The rate of return (*r* in the formula) significantly impacts outcomes, but higher returns typically involve increased volatility and risk. This tension between risk and reward requires investors, especially those starting small, to balance ambition with prudence. Indexed funds and diversified portfolios often offer steady, moderate growth conducive to long-term compounding. Through such vehicles, modest investors can access the broader market's benefits without incurring outsized risk—a practical application of the math of patience married to risk management principles.

Historical data reinforces this interplay. The S&P 500, for instance, has averaged a roughly 7% annual return after inflation over the past century, despite experiencing significant short-term downturns. Investors who weathered market fluctuations and maintained their investments reaped compounding benefits far exceeding the cumulative value of their contributions. This empirical reality demonstrates the resilience of patience against market volatility—a critical lesson for those susceptible to reactionary behaviours. The math of patience, thus, is not only a numerical truth but also an ethical appeal to long-term vision over short-term impulsivity.

Critically, the math of patience challenges the seductive narratives of financial speculation and rapid wealth accumulation. While stories of overnight success captivate, they represent outliers rather than norms. By grounding expectations in the disciplined accumulation afforded by compound interest, this approach advocates for sustainable financial growth rooted in realistic timeframes and consistent effort. This stance requires intellectual honesty about the slow, incremental nature of true wealth-building and fosters respect for the incremental victories that compose financial progress.

To translate theory into practice, the subchapter also examines strategies for embedding patience within one's financial habits. Automating investments to coincide with pay cycles ensures regular contributions without reliance on fluctuating motivation. Coupling savings goals with visual tracking reinforces progress and sustains engagement. Importantly, embracing the math of patience necessitates a mindset shift—from seeking immediate validation to appreciating gradual, compounding gains as markers of future freedom and security. This attitudinal transformation aligns behaviour with the mathematical realities, creating a virtuous cycle of consistent investment and growing confidence.

In sum, the math of patience is both a foundational principle and a transformative narrative within personal finance. It offers not only a path for those with limited means to build wealth but also a philosophical lens through which to view investing as an exercise in disciplined optimism. By appreciating the exponential growth that time facilitates, and integrating this understanding with behavioural strategies that foster long-term commitment, readers gain a powerful framework for approaching their financial futures. This subchapter, therefore, serves as both an intellectual and practical guide—revealing how tiny amounts, patient persistence, and informed choices converge to redefine what is possible in wealth accumulation.

Visualization over Calculation:

The abstraction of compound interest, percentages, and investment returns can often feel daunting, even alienating, particularly to those new to the world of finance. For many, the cold arithmetic of calculations offers little emotional resonance—numbers on a page rarely inspire the conviction necessary to sustain long-term investment behaviour. Yet, beneath the surface of these figures lies a transformative potential that, if properly visualised, can captivate the imagination and fuel sustained commitment. This subchapter asserts that *visualisation is not merely a pedagogical tool but a critical emotional bridge* between understanding and belief. By shifting focus from rote calculation to compelling visual representation, investors—especially those starting with modest sums—can internalise the promise of growth, fostering both motivation and patience.

To understand the power of visualisation, one might begin with cognitive psychology research, which reveals that the human brain processes images approximately 60,000 times faster than text or numbers. This neurological predisposition explains why charts, graphs, and infographics can evoke a visceral response that raw data seldom elicits. Consider the example of two investors presented with identical investment outcomes: one receives a spreadsheet showing incremental gains, while the other views a colourful growth curve illustrating exponential compounding. The latter is more likely to experience a concrete sense of progress and possibility. This illustrates a fundamental insight: *visual tools transform abstract numbers into relatable narratives of personal growth.*

Moreover, visualisation techniques can counteract the well-documented behavioural bias known as "present bias," where individuals disproportionately favour immediate rewards over future gains. When the future benefits of investing are hidden in distant, opaque numerical form, motivation wanes. Visual representations—such as progress bars tracking how close one is to a savings goal or dynamic charts depicting portfolio growth—make future rewards tangible and immediate in perception. For instance, digital investment platforms increasingly incorporate visual dashboards that show users not just how much money they have invested, but the trajectory of their wealth accumulation over time. This approach capitalises on the brain's affinity for patterns and milestones, making incremental progress psychologically rewarding.

Real-world applications of this principle abound. Take the case of Acorns, a micro-investing app that rounds up everyday purchases to the nearest pound and invests the spare change. Acorns uses visual cues—colourful pie charts, graphs, and milestone celebrations—to keep users engaged and motivated. The app's success among users with limited financial literacy and modest incomes underscores that *effective visualisation lowers barriers to entry and fosters a sustained saving mindset.* It is a potent reminder that the presentation of data is as critical as the data itself in building investor confidence and habit.

Yet, the relationship between visualisation and calculation need not be adversarial. Rather, *visual tools serve as complements to numerical literacy.* For example, financial advisors often employ scenario-based simulations to show clients how different investment decisions might play out under varying market conditions. These simulations combine quantitative rigor with accessible imagery, enabling investors to grasp complex concepts like risk diversification and market volatility without being overwhelmed. Thus, visualisation acts as a scaffold—supporting cognitive understanding while simultaneously nurturing emotional investment.

However, one must acknowledge potential pitfalls. Over-simplified or overly optimistic visualisations risk fostering unrealistic expectations. Graphs that assume fixed high rates of return without accounting for market variability can mislead and ultimately disillusion investors. Ethical design of visual tools demands transparency and contextualisation—clear annotations about assumptions, historical volatility, and the probabilistic nature of investment outcomes. This safeguards against the seductive allure of "perfect curves" and grounds visualisation in financial reality. A balanced approach cultivates informed optimism rather than blind faith.

The philosophical underpinning of this emphasis on visualisation rests on the recognition that *investing is as much a psychological endeavour as a mathematical one.* Numbers quantify capital growth, but beliefs and emotions drive behaviour. By engaging both hemispheres of the brain—the logical through calculation, the imaginative through visualisation—investors can achieve a harmonious understanding that propels action. This dual engagement is especially crucial for those whose financial journeys begin with small amounts, as the immediacy of visual progress helps sustain motivation during periods when numerical gains seem negligible.

In this light, the integration of visual tools into investing reflects a broader paradigm shift in personal finance education—from didactic instruction to experiential engagement. Interactive platforms, gamification elements, and personalized feedback loops transform passive observation into active participation. When investors see their micro-investments as growing gardens, rising staircases, or unfolding maps, the act of investing becomes a ritual imbued with meaning rather than a chore of bookkeeping. This transformation enhances emotional resilience, reduces anxiety, and encourages perseverance.

In practice, adopting visualization techniques involves more than using fancy apps or graphs. It requires *deliberate, repeated interaction with visual representations*—weekly reviews of progress, celebrating milestones, adjusting goals visually rather than solely numerically. For example, maintaining a visual journal or a digital dashboard that captures not just portfolio value but behavioural insights (such as consistency of contributions) fosters a holistic appreciation of the investing journey. Such practices create positive feedback loops where progress is visible, celebrated, and self-reinforcing.

Ultimately, the encouragement of visualization over pure calculation is a call to democratize investing. It recognises that financial literacy varies widely and that traditional approaches to personal finance often alienate rather than include. By meeting investors where they are—acknowledging cognitive diversity and emotional complexity—visual tools enable a broader spectrum of individuals to grasp, believe in, and commit to the slow but steady accumulation of wealth. The act of seeing one's financial future take shape visually is itself a powerful affirmation of agency, instilling hope and a sense of control.

This subchapter, therefore, serves as both a conceptual framework and a practical guide. It challenges readers to reconceptualise how they engage with their finances, proposing that *the real impact of investing unfolds not merely in calculations but in the cultivation of belief through visual narratives*. By embracing this approach, investors—regardless of their starting point—can develop the emotional stamina and cognitive clarity necessary for the enduring practice of building wealth over time.

Time as a Wealth Equalizer:

The persistent myth that beginning to invest late in life—or starting with modest sums—is a guaranteed financial failure persists stubbornly in popular culture and even within financial advice circles. This misconception, often rooted in a superficial reading of compound interest formulas and investment growth charts, can discourage countless individuals from engaging with investing altogether. Yet, a deeper exploration reveals that *time*, while undoubtedly an essential component of wealth accumulation, is far more nuanced in its role—acting as both an equaliser and an enabler rather than an unforgiving gatekeeper*. This subchapter seeks to dismantle the fatalism surrounding late or small starts and to illuminate how strategic, consistent investing, even from a delayed or limited position, can still cultivate meaningful financial resilience and growth.

Central to this reevaluation is a recognition that *wealth accumulation is not a race, but a system governed by the interplay of time, consistency, and compounding returns*. While it is true that early investors benefit from longer periods of compounding, the binary framing that 'starting late means failure' fails to account for practical realities such as income fluctuations, life transitions, and access disparities. Instead, it obscures the critical question: how can one leverage available time and resources most effectively, regardless of when investing begins? Here, the conversation shifts from lamenting lost time to embracing present opportunity with a pragmatic, forward-looking mindset.

Consider the illustrative example of someone beginning to invest at age 45, contributing modestly but regularly, compared to a peer who started at 25 but contributed inconsistently. The late starter, through disciplined saving and investment choices, can still amass a substantial portfolio by retirement, especially when investing in diversified, low-cost funds. This reality is supported by empirical studies; for instance, research from the National Bureau of Economic Research demonstrates that *consistent saving behaviours often outweigh the advantages of an early start when viewed over a multi-decade horizon.* Thus, the late starter's narrative can be one of empowerment rather than defeat.

The psychology of 'time as a wealth equalizer' also involves reframing *small contributions* not as inadequate but as foundational. The misconception that one must invest large sums immediately to succeed neglects the power of incremental growth. Investing $50 or even $10 monthly, if sustained, can accumulate into meaningful sums over 15 or 20 years. This challenges the prevailing 'all or nothing' attitude, positioning investment instead as an accessible process. The emphasis shifts to *habit formation and behavioural consistency*, which, research from behavioural economics reveals, are often stronger predictors of financial outcomes than initial capital alone.

Moreover, technological advances in finance democratise access to investing, further amplifying the potential for late or small investors. Fractional shares, micro-investing platforms, and automated contribution systems reduce barriers that historically favoured those with substantial capital and early market access. For example, platforms like Robinhood or Acorns allow incremental investments without prohibitive fees or minimum balances, thus enabling more equitable participation across age and income spectrums. These innovations underscore that *the temporal disadvantage of a late start can be mitigated by leveraging technology and smart investment vehicles.*

However, embracing time as a wealth equalizer does not mean ignoring risks or the realities of market volatility. The compressed time horizon of a late starter demands careful asset allocation, typically involving more conservative, diversified portfolios designed to balance growth with risk management. Strategic adjustments—such as dollar-cost averaging and regular portfolio rebalancing—can reduce exposure to market fluctuations, preserving capital while pursuing steady returns. This approach recognises that time interacts dynamically with investment strategy, necessitating adaptive decision-making rather than static adherence to early-investment paradigms.

Philosophically, the notion that it is 'too late to start' conflicts with broader understandings of agency and self-efficacy in personal finance. *Time is not a fixed, punitive measure but a resource whose value is contingent upon how it is engaged.* This perspective empowers investors to reclaim control over their financial narratives, fostering resilience in the face of past delays or limitations. It reframes investment as a process embedded within the broader arc of a person's life, where *each decision, regardless of timing, contributes to cumulative growth and security.*

Additionally, the cultural narratives around wealth and success often skew towards celebrating prodigies or early achievers, marginalising late bloomers and incrementalists. This bias reinforces exclusionary myths and overlooks the diversity of financial journeys. Highlighting stories of individuals who began investing later in life—such as entrepreneurs who redirected earnings from career shifts into retirement savings, or workers who capitalised on late-career bonuses—provides compelling counterexamples. These narratives demonstrate that *wealth-building is deeply personal and non-linear*, shaped by myriad factors beyond just chronological age.

Finally, the role of financial education in dismantling fatalistic attitudes towards time cannot be overstated. Clear, accessible teaching that emphasises *the cumulative power of consistent, patient investing* equips individuals to engage proactively, rather than despairingly, with their financial futures. Visual tools, scenario planning, and personalised goal setting foster a tangible sense of progress, even for those starting late or with limited means. Such education reframes time from an adversary into a collaborator in wealth-building.

In sum, *time as a wealth equalizer challenges entrenched myths by highlighting the transformative potential of sustained, informed investment behaviours regardless of starting point.* It insists on a paradigm where late or modest beginnings are not financial death sentences but invitations to engage with wealth-building in realistic, optimistic, and strategic ways. This subchapter invites readers to adopt a nuanced understanding of time's role—one that balances urgency with patience, capitalises on available resources, and nurtures an enduring commitment to financial agency.

The Moment You Feel It's Working:

There exists a moment in the investment journey that transcends numbers and charts—a moment when the abstract concept of 'growing wealth' becomes palpably real. It is the instant a person *feels* the payoff of their discipline, patience, and vision, an emotional turning point that validates effort and transforms investing from a distant goal into a lived experience. This subchapter explores these pivotal emotional milestones, unpacking why they matter as much as, if not more than, the financial figures themselves, and how recognising these moments can fuel sustained engagement and resilience in the long arc of wealth-building.

Financial progress is often measured in quantitative terms: portfolio balances, percentage returns, or compound interest calculations. Yet, this reductionist view overlooks a crucial psychological dimension. For many investors—especially those beginning with modest sums or from historically excluded backgrounds—the early phases of investing can feel intangible or even discouraging. The slow and incremental nature of compound growth makes immediate gratification rare. Without tangible emotional cues, the risk of disengagement or doubt grows. Recognising *when* and *how* an investor begins to sense genuine progress provides a vital counterweight to impatience and scepticism.

One illustrative real-world example is the experience of micro-investors who contribute as little as five pounds per week through apps like Acorns or Stash. For many, the first time they observe their investments outpacing what would have been left idle in a checking account can spark a profound shift. This is not merely a mathematical milestone; it represents *proof* of concept, a lived demonstration that small, consistent actions accumulate value. This emotional affirmation often catalyses deeper commitment and transforms saving and investing from abstract chores into acts of self-respect and empowerment.

These emotional turning points often correspond with what psychologists call *experiential learning*—moments when individuals connect cognitive understanding with personal experience. For example, receiving a quarterly statement showing unexpected gains, or witnessing reinvested dividends increase purchasing power, can trigger feelings of pride and ownership. Such events underscore the principle that *investing is as much a psychological endeavour as a financial one.* By highlighting these milestones, this subchapter encourages readers to tune into their emotional responses as meaningful signals on the path to financial maturity.

However, the emotional payoff is not exclusively positive or straightforward. Market fluctuations can produce anxiety or disillusionment, especially when initial enthusiasm confronts volatility. The ability to recognise *the moment it's genuinely working* amidst short-term noise requires both education and emotional intelligence. This includes understanding that *progress is non-linear* and that setbacks are intrinsic to the investment experience. A critical insight here is cultivating patience not just as a passive virtue but as an active engagement with uncertainty, one where emotional turning points reaffirm resilience rather than complacency.

Further complicating the narrative is the diversity of investor profiles and psychological thresholds. For a young professional, the moment might be crossing a personal savings target or seeing the first investment purchase. For a mid-career individual who starts late, it could be the first portfolio growth after years of cautious contributions. For retirees reallocating assets, the turning point might be stabilising income streams through dividends. This variety underscores that emotional payoffs are highly individualised and must be interpreted within personal context rather than universal benchmarks.

Technological innovations have introduced new ways to visualise and experience these milestones, enhancing emotional engagement. Gamified investment apps, progress dashboards, and personalised alerts provide continuous feedback loops that keep investors connected to their goals. These tools convert abstract figures into compelling narratives, helping users to *feel* their progress in real time. The integration of behavioural finance principles into technology design reflects an evolving understanding that *emotional reinforcement is essential for habit formation and long-term financial success.*

Yet, it is essential to distinguish genuine emotional turning points from fleeting dopamine hits generated by market hype or speculative trades. This subchapter explores how to identify moments rooted in *building sustainable value* rather than emotional adrenaline. Recognising this difference protects investors from burnout and impulsive decisions that can undermine financial wellbeing. It encourages a mindset where emotional payoffs support strategic discipline and not short-term gratification.

Ethical reflection also enters this discussion. The celebration of emotional milestones must not obscure systemic inequalities that constrain financial agency for many. This awareness grounds the emotional narrative within a broader social context, reminding readers that *individual turning points are both personal victories and potential catalysts for collective empowerment.* Embracing emotional payoffs as markers of progress contributes to dismantling the fatalism that often accompanies financial exclusion.

Ultimately, the moment investors feel it's working marks a *threshold of transformation*, bridging the gap between aspiration and achievement. It is an inflection point where investing ceases to be a mere task and becomes an integral part of identity and future orientation. This subchapter equips readers to recognise and cultivate these moments, nurturing emotional engagement that sustains them through the inevitable challenges ahead. In doing so, it affirms that *true financial empowerment is as much about feeling as it is about calculating—about owning one's story as much as one's assets.*

Chapter 9
Wealth as a Cultural Rebellion

The stories we inherit about money—shaped by family, community, and social circumstance—exert a quiet but formidable influence over how we perceive wealth and our capacity to attain it. These narratives are seldom neutral; more often than not, they carry the weight of generational struggle, systemic inequities, and class boundaries that frame economic access as predetermined. Yet embedded within these inherited stories lies the possibility for profound transformation. This chapter positions wealth not merely as an individual pursuit but as a form of cultural defiance—an assertion of agency against systems that have long sought to marginalise entire communities through exclusion from economic opportunity. Even modest acts of investing can function as subtle yet potent declarations of presence and self-determination.

Take, for instance, the decision to invest twenty-five dollars. On the surface, this might appear inconsequential. But within the broader context of systemic barriers, such an act becomes a deliberate statement: a refusal to remain invisible. It marks participation in an ongoing assertion of economic presence, a claim on futures that history has often denied. In this light, investment is no longer merely transactional; it assumes symbolic resonance, challenging inherited assumptions that certain groups are permanently outside the domain of financial influence or capability.

The chapter further explores the delicate balance between visibility and comparison. Sharing one's financial journey can inspire and empower—or, conversely, trigger shame when measured against unrealistic benchmarks of wealth and success. Here, frameworks are presented to support progress that is recognised authentically, privately or publicly, without succumbing to competitive pressures. This approach elevates self-recognition over comparison, validating diverse financial experiences while fostering a culture of dignity and communal encouragement rather than judgment.

Equally vital is the principle of "teaching from the middle, not the summit." Conventional financial advice often emanates from the pinnacle of wealth, creating a gap between guidance and lived experience for those still navigating foundational steps. This chapter advocates for mentors and guides who lead from intermediate stages of financial growth, demonstrating practical insight rooted in real-world challenges. Such a perspective democratises knowledge, framing readers as active participants in a collective journey, capable of inspiring others through evolving experience rather than distant ideals.

Throughout, attention is given to the structural forces shaping wealth access. Success is not romanticised as purely individual achievement; it is situated within broader considerations of social justice and economic equity. By framing wealth as a vehicle for cultural resistance, readers are encouraged to view their financial choices as entwined with historical narratives and communal aspirations. Wealth-building thus emerges as a multifaceted act—affirming identity, resisting systemic exclusion, and cultivating legacies for future generations.

Interwoven with these ideas are real-world examples of individuals and communities embodying this ethos. Small acts of saving and investing ripple outward, creating networks of mutual support, mentorship, and inspiration. These narratives illuminate dimensions of financial life often overlooked in traditional discourse—the emotional, symbolic, and socially generative aspects of wealth accumulation. They reinforce the understanding that empowerment involves reclaiming dignity and agency as much as accruing capital.

Ultimately, this chapter equips readers with the intellectual frameworks and emotional tools necessary to reimagine their relationship with money. It challenges inherited assumptions, encourages critical reflection, and fosters a vision of wealth that extends beyond personal gain into cultural transformation. By situating financial literacy within a broader narrative of empowerment, justice, and shared progress, it presents wealth as a dynamic, collective force capable of shaping not only individual futures but also the legacies of entire communities.

Money Stories We Inherit:

Money is more than currency; it is a language shaped by stories passed down through generations, stories that form the very framework of our relationship with wealth, scarcity, and opportunity. These inherited narratives—woven through family histories, racial identities, and class experiences—shape not only how individuals approach money but also how entire communities navigate economic systems. To understand financial behaviour today, one must first unpack these deep-rooted money stories, which are as much about culture and identity as they are about numbers and budgets. This exploration reveals the profound ways in which money narratives act as both barriers and bridges in the quest for financial empowerment.

Generational money stories carry the imprint of historical circumstances, often reflecting cycles of opportunity and trauma. For many, family discussions around money are scarce or shrouded in anxiety, secrecy, or even shame. Take, for instance, the legacy of immigrant families whose financial behaviours are informed by past deprivations or survival in unstable environments. Stories of "making do" with less, or the fear of debt and loss, become embedded in attitudes toward spending, saving, and investing. These narratives influence decision-making long after the initial hardship has passed, creating a psychological inheritance that conditions financial habits, risk tolerance, and even self-worth. An individual's reluctance to invest may stem not simply from lack of knowledge but from inherited caution encoded in familial experience.

Racial money narratives add another layer of complexity, shaped by systemic exclusion and economic discrimination. The economic realities faced by communities of colour are not only products of individual choices but of structural inequities embedded within policy, law, and social practice. The racial wealth gap, for example, is more than statistics—it is a lived reality steeped in generational disenfranchisement, redlining, employment discrimination, and unequal access to education and capital. These collective experiences give rise to money stories marked by resilience but also by skepticism toward financial institutions historically exploitative or inaccessible. The narrative of scarcity in these contexts often intertwines with broader struggles for dignity and recognition, making financial empowerment both a personal and political act.

Class-based narratives further influence how money is understood and managed. Economic class conditions the vocabulary of financial possibility, shaping what is perceived as attainable or realistic. For working-class families, money stories frequently centre on survival—prioritising immediate needs over long-term wealth-building, viewing debt as an unavoidable tool, and seeing investment as a distant or elitist concept. Conversely, middle- and upper-class money stories often assume a baseline of stability and access that makes planning and investing routine parts of life. This divergence in narratives creates differing relationships with financial advice and the systems designed to support wealth accumulation. Recognising class-based money stories exposes the implicit assumptions in mainstream financial guidance and underscores the necessity of culturally and economically nuanced approaches.

Contrasting these inherited narratives are emergent stories that challenge and reshape the relationship with money. Financial literacy movements and community-based initiatives increasingly highlight stories of agency and transformation. These narratives do not ignore structural barriers but rather situate individual and collective financial actions within contexts of resistance and innovation. For example, the rise of micro-investing platforms has sparked new stories around inclusion—offering ways to participate in wealth-building regardless of starting capital. Similarly, storytelling in financial education now often emphasises the reframing of money as a tool for self-determination rather than a source of shame or anxiety.

Critical to this reframing is the acknowledgement of emotional and ethical dimensions within money stories. Money is inseparable from identity, power, and belonging, and financial decisions carry emotional weight that can reinforce or dismantle limiting narratives. An ethical reflection on money stories encourages readers to interrogate not only their inherited beliefs but also the broader societal narratives perpetuated through media, education, and policy. It invites a nuanced understanding that financial empowerment is as much about healing and reclamation as it is about arithmetic and strategy.

Case studies illustrate the potency of money stories and their evolution. Consider families who, despite histories of economic hardship, cultivate narratives that foreground resilience, intergenerational support, and strategic risk-taking. These stories reveal how new financial behaviours—such as regular saving, investing, and financial planning—are not simply practical shifts but symbolic acts of redefining identity and possibility. They demonstrate the interplay between inherited narratives and intentional change, highlighting that financial transformation often requires rewriting one's money story.

In unpacking generational, racial, and class-based money narratives, this chapter emphasises specificity over generalisation. It resists simplistic dichotomies of 'poor versus rich' or 'knowledge versus ignorance' and instead presents a layered, context-rich understanding of how money stories function. This approach honours the diversity of experiences and acknowledges that financial behaviour is embedded in complex social and psychological matrices.

Ultimately, recognising the money stories we inherit is the first step toward conscious financial agency. It equips readers to see beyond the surface of budgets and investment plans to the deeper scripts that shape their economic lives. This awareness fosters empathy—for oneself and others—and lays the groundwork for building new narratives that support equity, dignity, and sustainable wealth-building. As readers engage with this critical analysis, they are invited to become not only wiser financial actors but also storytellers who actively shape the culture of wealth for generations to come.

The Quiet Politics of $25:

Investing a mere twenty-five dollars might seem insignificant within the vast, often intimidating world of finance. Yet, beneath this modest sum lies a profound act of defiance—a quiet, deliberate refusal to be erased by economic exclusion. The politics of $25 extends far beyond numbers and market returns; it is an emblem of agency, belonging, and resistance for those historically marginalized by financial systems designed to keep them at the periphery. To grasp the true power of such a small investment is to understand how economic participation functions not only as a pathway to wealth but as a mode of cultural and political reclamation.

At the heart of this quiet politics is the recognition that financial exclusion is both systemic and symbolic. Historically, entire communities—often delineated by race, class, or geography—have faced deliberate barriers to wealth-building tools: limited access to banking, discriminatory lending practices, and exclusion from investment opportunities. These mechanisms operate not merely as economic hurdles but as instruments of social invisibility, signalling to excluded groups that their economic participation is neither expected nor welcome. Investing even a token amount becomes a radical act because it interrupts this narrative of erasure, affirming presence in a system that often denies it.

The emergence of micro-investing platforms and fractional shares has reshaped the contours of this political landscape. Platforms like Acorns, Stash, and others allow users to invest spare change, breaking down traditional financial gatekeeping. For someone with limited disposable income, a $25 investment may be their first step into the realm of investing—a step that carries outsized psychological and cultural significance. This is not simply about financial returns but about cultivating a new identity: one of investor rather than excluded outsider. Such tools democratise access but also symbolise a shift in who belongs in conversations about wealth, security, and economic futures.

Importantly, the act of investing small sums is deeply intertwined with notions of dignity and self-determination. Economic exclusion often strips individuals not only of material resources but also of the dignity associated with participation in mainstream economic life. Making a choice to invest—even modestly—asserts control over one's financial narrative. It transforms money from a source of anxiety into a lever of empowerment. This shift, while subtle, can cascade into broader confidence, encouraging more deliberate saving, budgeting, and engagement with financial education. The politics of $25 is thus also a politics of self-empowerment through incremental action.

Critically, this act must be understood within a broader social and ethical context. While celebrating the power of small investments, it is vital to resist narratives that place the onus solely on individuals to overcome systemic barriers through personal grit. The quiet politics of $25 is not a panacea for structural inequality; rather, it is a symbolic disruption within a landscape that requires far-reaching reform. Recognising this distinction prevents the romanticisation of small-scale investing as a substitute for addressing economic injustice at its roots. It situates the act as both a personal assertion and a call for systemic change.

The cultural resonance of investing small amounts also challenges dominant paradigms of wealth as the province of the wealthy or financially savvy. By embracing and valuing modest participation, communities can rewrite money stories that have long been characterised by scarcity and exclusion. This shift fosters an inclusive financial culture where success is not defined solely by large-scale accumulation but by sustained engagement and intergenerational progress. The politics of $25 invites a recalibration of what financial participation means and whom it serves.

Case studies illustrate the transformative potential of this reframing. Consider community-driven investment groups that pool small contributions to build collective wealth or individuals from underserved communities who use micro-investing as an entry point into broader economic literacy and confidence. These examples illuminate how small-scale investing can generate ripple effects beyond individual portfolios—strengthening social bonds, fostering financial resilience, and cultivating a shared sense of economic agency.

Yet, the politics of $25 also entails tensions and contradictions. The financial industry's embrace of micro-investing platforms raises questions about commodification and consumer protection. Are these platforms truly tools of empowerment, or do they mask exploitative practices under the guise of accessibility? Readers must engage critically with these questions, balancing optimism about democratization with vigilance against new forms of economic precarity.

Moreover, there is a psychological dimension to consider. The visibility of one's modest investment can evoke vulnerability, particularly in environments where financial success is often measured by scale. This tension underscores the importance of cultivating narratives that normalise and celebrate incremental progress, fostering communities where every act of investment, no matter the size, is recognised as a meaningful stride toward economic inclusion.

Ultimately, the politics embedded in a $25 investment transcends the transactional. It is a statement against invisibility, a quiet but potent refusal to accept marginalisation. This subchapter invites readers to appreciate the profound significance of small-scale financial participation as an act of cultural rebellion and economic affirmation. It encourages a nuanced understanding of how modest investments intersect with histories of exclusion, contemporary financial innovations, and the ongoing struggle for equity and dignity in economic life. Through this lens, $25 is not merely a dollar amount—it is a threshold where personal empowerment and collective transformation begin.

Visibility without Comparison:

Visibility is a double-edged sword. The act of sharing one's financial journey—whether with close friends, wider social circles, or anonymous online communities—can foster connection, accountability, and encouragement. Yet visibility can also expose individuals to comparison, judgment, and shame, particularly in a culture that equates financial worth with social value. The challenge lies not in choosing whether to be visible, but in learning how to share authentically and constructively without falling prey to the corrosive effects of comparison. This balance, often overlooked in personal finance discourse, is essential for sustaining motivation and cultivating a healthy relationship with money.

Sharing financial progress publicly or privately serves various important psychological and social functions. It can demystify investing and saving, reducing feelings of isolation and reinforcing a sense of agency. For example, numerous online communities dedicated to budgeting, debt repayment, or investing demonstrate how collective visibility fosters mutual learning and support. Individuals recount small victories—paying off a credit card, making a first investment—that might otherwise seem insignificant. These shared narratives create a culture where incremental progress is recognised and celebrated, countering pervasive societal pressures for immediate, spectacular success. Visibility, in this sense, can be a radical act of normalisation and empowerment.

Yet the social dynamics of sharing are fraught with pitfalls. The ubiquitous presence of curated success stories on social media platforms can engender unhealthy comparisons, leading to feelings of inadequacy and discouragement. When financial progress is showcased only in terms of milestones or net worth, it obscures the diverse and nonlinear realities many face. For those with less financial privilege, public visibility might inadvertently reinforce stigma, as their experiences deviate from dominant narratives of upward mobility. This underscores the necessity of cultivating a form of visibility that is intentionally decoupled from competitive comparison—a visibility rooted in personal context and vulnerability.

Practically, this demands a reframing of what it means to share financial information. Visibility without comparison begins with recognising that every individual's financial path is shaped by unique circumstances: income variability, family obligations, access to education, and systemic barriers. By embracing this complexity, sharers and audiences alike can move beyond binary judgments of success or failure. Instead, sharing becomes an act of storytelling that honours process over outcome. For example, a person might share the discipline it took to automate a modest savings plan despite irregular income, or the emotional work involved in overcoming financial anxiety. These narratives invite empathy and nuance, fostering an environment where diverse experiences are validated rather than ranked.

Another critical element is the choice of audience and medium. Visibility need not always mean broadcasting to a vast audience; it can be a quiet practice of journaling or sharing within trusted circles. Private financial journals or apps that encourage reflection without external exposure can serve as safe spaces for tracking progress free from social comparison. Alternatively, participating in peer support groups—whether in person or online—allows for shared vulnerability within a contained, empathetic community. Such spaces balance the benefits of visibility with protection against the pitfalls of comparison and judgment, enabling sustained engagement with one's financial goals.

Moreover, cultivating visibility without comparison entails adopting a language of self-compassion and growth. Financial journeys are often punctuated by setbacks, and the pressure to present an unblemished narrative can inhibit authenticity. When individuals learn to frame challenges not as failures but as integral components of growth, sharing becomes a tool for resilience rather than shame. This mindset shift is supported by psychological research indicating that self-compassion mitigates the negative emotional impact of setbacks and promotes persistence. Communicating this attitude in shared stories normalises imperfection and encourages others to approach their financial lives with kindness and patience.

There are ethical considerations in how financial journeys are shared publicly. Transparency about context—such as sources of income, levels of debt, or financial support networks—helps prevent misleading impressions that might foster envy or disillusionment. Public figures and influencers in the personal finance space bear responsibility for representing diverse realities and avoiding narratives that unintentionally marginalise or alienate their audiences. Ethical visibility models equity and inclusivity, recognising the power dynamics embedded in financial discourse and striving to democratise knowledge and confidence.

Importantly, visibility without comparison is not merely a personal or interpersonal strategy but a cultural imperative. It challenges dominant narratives that valorise wealth accumulation as a zero-sum game and instead promotes communal well-being and shared learning. By shifting the conversation from competition to collaboration, financial visibility can contribute to dismantling stigma around money struggles and create pathways for collective empowerment. This is especially critical in addressing economic disparities that disproportionately affect historically marginalised communities.

The practice of sharing financial journeys in ways that resist comparison also intersects with broader themes of identity and self-worth. Financial visibility becomes a site for reconstructing one's relationship with money—not as a measure of personal value but as a tool for achieving meaningful life goals. When individuals reclaim their narratives on their own terms, visibility empowers autonomy and self-definition. This internal shift is often the catalyst for sustained behavioural change and deeper engagement with financial health.

Ultimately, visibility without comparison invites a recalibration of how we understand and enact financial sharing. It requires conscious effort to foreground context, vulnerability, and empathy, transforming sharing from a performance into a dialogue. This approach enables individuals to leverage the motivational benefits of visibility while safeguarding their emotional well-being. For readers embarking on or continuing their financial journeys, mastering this balance is essential to turning visibility into a source of strength rather than a trigger for shame.

Through real-world examples, psychological insights, and ethical reflection, this subchapter offers readers practical frameworks and mindset shifts to share their financial stories with confidence and compassion. It illuminates a path toward financial transparency that uplifts rather than divides, fostering communities where every journey is respected and every voice heard without the shadow of comparison. In doing so, it affirms the transformative potential of visibility—not as a spectacle, but as a connective, empowering practice rooted in honesty and mutual support.

Teaching Others from the Middle, Not the Top:

To teach from the middle rather than the top is to embrace a mode of guidance rooted in authenticity, relatability, and humility. It challenges traditional hierarchies of knowledge and authority that place so-called experts on pedestals, often creating unbridgeable gaps between those who have achieved financial mastery and those still navigating their way. This approach acknowledges that expertise is not a prerequisite for leadership in financial education; rather, it is the willingness to share lived experience, to model vulnerability, and to foster community learning that cultivates true influence. In a landscape saturated with polished financial advice and unreachable benchmarks, teaching from the middle offers a more inclusive, accessible, and ultimately transformative path.

The premise that one must be an expert before sharing financial knowledge is not only exclusionary but counterproductive. Expertise often connotes mastery and perfection—conditions that many readers have yet to achieve or may never fully attain given the complexity and variability of personal finance. Teaching from the middle recognises that the process of learning and growing financially is ongoing and non-linear. This reframing aligns with contemporary educational psychology, which emphasises "growth mindsets" and peer-to-peer learning as powerful mechanisms for behavioural change. The guide is not the infallible authority but a fellow traveller who shares practical insights and emotional truths drawn from navigating challenges and setbacks, not just successes.

Real-world examples abound of individuals who have embraced this role with remarkable impact. Consider the rise of personal finance bloggers and social media influencers whose appeal lies precisely in their candidness about imperfection. They share budgeting struggles, debt repayment milestones, and investment experiments, fostering a sense of shared journey rather than distant ideal. Their followers are not passive recipients but active participants, learning through communal dialogue rather than top-down instruction. This model disrupts the traditional dynamic and suggests that teaching effectiveness is amplified when guides are transparent about their financial realities.

Teaching from the middle also addresses the pervasive issue of financial intimidation. Many people hesitate to seek or share financial advice due to fear of judgment or feelings of inadequacy. When guidance comes from those who are visibly engaged in the same process, it normalises imperfection and invites curiosity rather than fear. This lowers barriers to entry and encourages experimentation—two essential conditions for financial growth. The shared experience becomes a catalyst for empowerment, illustrating that progress is possible regardless of starting point or background.

However, teaching from the middle requires intentionality and self-awareness. It demands that guides cultivate credibility through honesty, empathy, and evidence-based reasoning rather than relying on credentials or status. The responsibility lies in balancing personal narrative with sound financial principles, avoiding the pitfalls of anecdotal overreach or prescriptive certainty. For instance, a guide might share how they managed fluctuating income streams or navigated credit challenges while also contextualising these experiences within broader financial literacy frameworks. This hybrid approach honours complexity and avoids simplistic solutions.

Ethically, teaching from the middle confronts power imbalances endemic to financial advice. It challenges the often exploitative "expert" culture that commodifies financial knowledge, sometimes alienating those who cannot afford professional services. Instead, it envisions a democratized pedagogy where knowledge flows horizontally and financial agency is a shared project. This ethic resonates deeply in communities historically marginalised by mainstream finance, where distrust of traditional institutions persists. Peer-led guidance can reestablish trust and cultural relevance, making financial education not just informative but transformative.

Moreover, becoming a guide from the middle expands the definition of financial leadership. It embraces relational influence, where change occurs through dialogue, shared values, and mutual accountability. This contrasts with transactional or didactic models and aligns with contemporary understandings of social capital and behavioural economics. The guide acts as a social signal, embodying attainable success and resilience, which motivates others through identification rather than aspiration. Such leadership is sustainable and scalable, leveraging community networks rather than individual prowess.

In practice, guiding from the middle involves a repertoire of skills beyond financial knowledge: active listening, storytelling, framing failure as learning, and facilitating group reflection. These competencies transform financial conversations into spaces of psychological safety, where vulnerability is met with encouragement rather than critique. The guide's role is less to instruct and more to accompany, modelling curiosity and adaptability. This relational approach is especially vital given the emotional dimensions of money—fear, shame, hope—that often impede progress.

Importantly, this approach does not diminish the value of expert advice but situates it within a broader ecosystem. Experts provide foundational knowledge and technical insights, but the lived, nuanced, and contextualised guidance from peers complements and humanises abstract concepts. The middle-ground guide acts as a bridge, translating theory into practice and connecting diverse experiences. This synthesis enhances comprehension and motivates sustained engagement with financial goals.

For readers contemplating how to contribute their own financial experiences to others' learning, the invitation is to begin where they are, with what they know, and how they have grown. Authenticity, not perfection, is the currency of influence. By sharing struggles and incremental wins, guides demystify financial progress and inspire actionable hope. This democratization of teaching encourages more voices to enter the conversation, enriching the collective wisdom available to all.

In sum, teaching others from the middle rather than the top reframes financial guidance as a shared journey rather than a hierarchical transmission. It emphasises connection over credentials, process over perfection, and empowerment over authority. This model realigns financial education with principles of equity, empathy, and community, ultimately fostering deeper, more enduring change. For those ready to lead not as experts but as exemplars, this approach offers both a practical framework and a profound call to action

Chapter 10
The Wealth Practice—Living the Identity, Not Just the Numbers

Wealth is too often reduced to rows on a balance sheet, a tally of transactions, or a distant target defined by milestones. Yet beneath these numerical measures lies something far richer: wealth as a lived experience, a form of identity expressed through daily choices, habits, and inner narratives. This chapter invites readers to move beyond the arithmetic of accumulation and to inhabit wealth as a state of being—to assume the posture, mindset, and rituals of an investor not occasionally, but as a defining element of selfhood. When viewed this way, investing shifts from a mechanical task into a ritual, and from a remote aspiration into a present, embodied practice.

Investing thus becomes inseparable from how one values oneself in the moment. Rituals, no matter how modest, carry disproportionate power in shaping identity. They create continuity between intention and action, rendering the abstract idea of "investor" tangible through repetition and presence. Whether it's reviewing a portfolio with deliberate focus, setting aside a small sum with quiet resolve, or reaffirming one's financial agency each morning, these daily acts embed investment into the fabric of life. Their potency derives not from spectacle but from consistency and mindfulness.

Equally vital is the bridge between present and future selves. Future pacing—a technique drawn from narrative psychology—helps readers visualise their financial futures not as abstract or distant, but as integral chapters in their personal story. Aligning today's actions with tomorrow's aspirations dissolves the dissonance that often undermines long-term engagement, creating motivation anchored in identity rather than obligation. By weaving past experiences, present commitments, and future goals into a coherent narrative, readers are positioned as active participants in their financial journey, rather than passive observers of circumstance.

This chapter also confronts entrenched beliefs about legitimacy and permission in investing. The statement "you are no longer a bystander" functions as both challenge and invitation: investing is not reserved for the wealthy, credentialed, or formally trained. The role of investor can be claimed by anyone, regardless of portfolio size or expertise. In doing so, authority shifts inward, empowering readers to ground their financial actions in conviction rather than external validation.

To consolidate this transformation, the chapter introduces a practical framework for cultivating a living wealth philosophy—a dynamic manifesto that evolves with experience. This Wealth Manifesto captures personal values, financial objectives, and guiding strategies, inviting reflection on ethics, emotional relationships to money, and the broader impact of financial decisions. By articulating a coherent philosophy, readers can anchor their practice in purpose and resilience, navigating the uncertainties of markets and life with clarity.

Throughout, the discussion draws on real-world examples and interdisciplinary insights—from behavioural economics and psychology to cultural studies—to illuminate the deep interplay between identity and financial behaviour. Wealth is framed not merely as accumulation but as an ongoing process of self-construction, expressed through choices, habits, and mindset. By embracing this perspective, readers are encouraged to see the cultivation of a wealth identity as a form of wealth in its own right.

By the chapter's conclusion, readers emerge with more than knowledge; they gain a toolkit for embodying wealth in everyday life. Investing is reimagined as a practice of self-authorship, where alignment with one's values and future becomes as central as any numerical goal. Wealth, in this conception, is not simply amassed; it is lived, intentional, and inseparable from the identity of the individual who cultivates it.

Wealth Is a Daily Attitude:

Wealth is often misunderstood as a distant goal, a numerical target etched on spreadsheets or financial statements. Yet beneath this external tally lies a more subtle, enduring reality: wealth as a *daily attitude*, an ongoing commitment expressed through ritualised behaviour and sustained identity. This distinction is not trivial. To inhabit the identity of an investor is to enact it consistently—through small acts and rituals that reinforce one's financial agency, rather than waiting passively for arbitrary milestones to define success. Wealth is not only what you accumulate, but how you show up to your financial life every single day.

At its core, cultivating a wealth identity means embedding financial intention into the rhythms of daily existence. The habitual nature of rituals makes abstract aspirations concrete. Consider the power of seemingly modest acts: setting aside a modest sum each month, reviewing one's portfolio with attentive curiosity, or simply reading a brief financial article over morning coffee. These acts serve as anchors, affirming the investor role repeatedly and subtly. Neuroscience suggests that repeated behaviour physically rewires neural pathways, making the investor identity not just a cognitive concept but a lived reality. *Wealth becomes a state of being, not just a destination.*

This perspective challenges dominant cultural narratives that equate wealth with sudden windfalls or outsized gains. Such narratives often foster impatience and frustration, obscuring the reality that *steady, incremental investment behaviour* is the primary engine of lasting financial growth. The ethos of "all or nothing" is replaced by a pragmatic embrace of continuity, underscoring how rituals—no matter how small—compound over time into formidable financial advantage. This approach resonates with behavioural economics, which shows that frequent, low-friction actions tend to produce better long-term adherence than rare, high-effort interventions.

The psychological dimension of wealth as a daily attitude is equally important. When investors ritualise their engagement with finances, they cultivate resilience against the market's inevitable volatility and the emotional turbulence it can provoke. Rituals provide stability and predictability amidst uncertainty, reducing cognitive load and emotional overwhelm. This is not to say rituals guarantee immunity to setbacks, but rather that they embed a disciplined mindset that frames setbacks as temporary and manageable. *Financial identity forged through ritual supports adaptive responses rather than reactive panic.*

Practical application of this philosophy can take many forms, each tailored to individual circumstances and preferences. Some may create a "financial morning routine" that includes reviewing budgets, market updates, and setting investment intentions. Others might schedule a weekly "investment reflection"—a deliberate pause to assess portfolio alignment with personal goals, independent of market noise. The key is consistency and meaningful engagement rather than rigid formality. These rituals should feel integrated, not burdensome, fostering a sense of ownership and curiosity.

Real-world examples abound of individuals transforming their financial lives through ritualised behaviour. Consider a young professional who commits to automatic monthly transfers to a retirement account, viewing this as a non-negotiable act of self-respect rather than a chore. Or a middle-aged investor who journals monthly about their financial progress, articulating lessons learned and recalibrating goals, turning abstract numbers into a living narrative. These practices nurture not only financial literacy but a psychological commitment that transcends fluctuations in net worth.

It is also necessary to examine potential tensions in ritualising wealth identity. Over-identification with financial metrics can risk reducing self-worth to portfolio value, an unhealthy conflation that rituals must consciously avoid reinforcing. Hence, rituals should be embedded within a broader framework of values and purpose, situating wealth as a means to meaningful ends rather than an end itself. Integrating reflective practices—such as periodic reassessment of what wealth means personally and ethically—can mitigate the risk of ritual becoming mechanical or isolating.

Moreover, rituals in wealth-building carry ethical and social dimensions. Financial behaviours ripple outward, influencing family, community, and broader social systems. Ritualised transparency, for example, can encourage dialogue about money within families, demystifying finance and breaking cycles of secrecy or shame. Similarly, community-oriented rituals—such as group investment clubs or peer accountability circles—can amplify commitment while fostering mutual support and learning. Wealth, as a daily attitude, thus becomes a shared cultural practice rather than an individualistic pursuit.

In contemporary contexts where digital tools and platforms proliferate, technology can enhance the ritualisation of investing. Automated contributions, personalised financial dashboards, and timely reminders scaffold daily engagement, reducing friction and reinforcing habit formation. Yet technology is a tool, not a substitute for intention. Ritual remains a conscious act of meaning-making, not a passive byproduct of automation. The interplay between human agency and technological facilitation is a vital consideration in designing sustainable wealth practices.

This subchapter seeks to deepen understanding of wealth not as a static achievement but as a dynamic identity continually enacted through ritual. It challenges readers to rethink their relationship with money, from passive management to active embodiment. By cultivating rituals aligned with personal values and goals, investors can foster resilience, continuity, and meaning in their financial lives. The real power of wealth lies not in the sums amassed but in the *daily decisions that shape who you are as an investor and, ultimately, as a steward of your future.*

Every act of financial engagement, no matter how small, carries the potential to affirm your identity as an investor. These acts ripple outward, building confidence and coherence that weather market cycles and life's unpredictability. The daily attitude of wealth is a practice—one that invites commitment, curiosity, and a profound sense of agency. This article offers a framework to integrate such rituals thoughtfully and sustainably, transforming the often intimidating world of investing into a personal journey of growth and empowerment.

Integrating Your Financial Self with Your Future Self:

Financial decisions, particularly those involving investment and saving, often fall victim to a profound temporal disconnect: the self in the present moment struggles to reconcile with the self that will inhabit the future. This tension—between immediate gratification and long-term benefit—is as much psychological as it is financial. The notion of *integrating your financial self with your future self* seeks to resolve this dissonance by employing future pacing and narrative design as strategic tools to bridge today's actions with tomorrow's identity. This integration is not a peripheral idea but a foundational practice for sustaining disciplined financial behaviour and meaningful wealth building over time.

At the heart of this challenge lies a cognitive bias known as temporal discounting, where individuals disproportionately value immediate rewards over delayed ones. Classic experiments in behavioural economics reveal how this bias undermines saving and investing, leading many to defer or abandon prudent financial planning. Yet, emerging research underscores that this bias is not fixed; it can be softened by enhancing the salience and emotional connection to the future self. When people vividly imagine and identify with their future selves, they exhibit stronger commitment to decisions that favour long-term wellbeing. *Future pacing*, a concept borrowed from psychotherapy and behavioural science, involves mentally projecting oneself into a future scenario where the consequences of current choices become tangible, thereby realigning motivation and behaviour in the present.

Narrative design complements future pacing by framing financial decisions as part of an ongoing personal story rather than isolated transactions. Humans are inherently narrative creatures; we organise experience through stories that construct coherent identities over time. Constructing a financial narrative that links current actions to future goals fosters continuity of self and imbues otherwise mundane financial tasks with purpose. For example, envisioning monthly contributions to a retirement fund as chapters in a story of financial independence transforms saving from an abstract obligation into a meaningful rite of passage. This narrative reframing encourages persistence and resilience, especially during periods of market volatility or personal hardship.

The practical application of these insights can be seen in techniques that encourage vivid, personalised envisioning of the future. Financial advisors and coaches often guide clients through exercises that involve writing detailed letters from their future selves, imagining their lifestyle, values, and challenges at retirement or other milestones. This process deepens empathy with the future self and crystallises motivations. Such exercises reveal that the future self is not a distant abstraction but a continuous extension of the present self, deserving of care and respect. The act of crafting these narratives transforms abstract goals into concrete aspirations, heightening accountability and emotional investment.

Real-world case studies reinforce the power of this approach. Research published in the *Journal of Experimental Psychology* demonstrated that participants who interacted with digital avatars resembling their future selves were more likely to allocate greater sums to saving than those without such cues. Similarly, financial planning apps incorporating features that visualise future balances, potential life scenarios, or projected income streams help users concretise abstract numbers into relatable futures. These tools harness the brain's predilection for stories and imagery, making the future feel immediate and actionable.

Yet, this process also invites reflection on ethical and psychological complexities. The future is inherently uncertain, and over identification with an idealised future self risks disappointment or rigidity if reality diverges from expectation. Therefore, integration demands a balance: cultivating a future-oriented identity while retaining flexibility and self-compassion in the face of setbacks. The narrative should be living and evolving, not dogmatic. This stance fosters adaptive behaviour and mitigates the paralysis that sometimes arises from perfectionism or fear of failure.

Moreover, the cultural and socio-economic contexts in which individuals operate shape their access to future pacing and narrative design practices. Marginalised groups often inherit financial narratives marked by scarcity, mistrust, or exclusion, complicating the integration of future selves with present actions. Addressing these structural barriers requires not only individual psychological work but also systemic change to democratise access to financial education, tools, and resources. The narrative of wealth-building must therefore expand beyond individualism to include collective dimensions of empowerment and justice.

In the intersection of identity, psychology, and finance, integrating one's financial self with one's future self emerges as a crucial practice. It transforms financial decision-making from a fragmented, transactional experience into a coherent, embodied journey. This integration fosters behavioural consistency, resilience, and purpose, enabling individuals to inhabit their role as investors and savers with authenticity and conviction. *The narrative arc of wealth creation becomes not merely about numbers amassed but about the continuous evolution of self across time.*

The practical implications are profound. By adopting future pacing and narrative design, readers gain access to cognitive and emotional tools that bolster long-term financial health. They learn to reframe financial discipline as an act of self-care and identity affirmation, rather than sacrifice or burden. They cultivate patience, perspective, and motivation, essential virtues in the inherently uncertain landscape of investment and wealth accumulation. This subchapter will offer concrete strategies and reflections to guide readers in weaving a personal financial narrative that harmonises present actions with future aspirations, ultimately bridging the psychological gap that so often impedes effective wealth building.

You Are No Longer a Bystander:

Claiming the identity of investor is no longer a privilege reserved for the few, nor is it contingent on a grand entry point of capital or prior financial achievement. *You are no longer a bystander*—this declaration cuts through decades of cultural gatekeeping and psychological hesitation that have relegated many to the sidelines of wealth creation. To embrace the role of investor today demands neither permission nor proof of success; it requires a shift in mindset, an understanding that the very act of participation—regardless of scale—is a transformative assertion of agency and belonging.

The historical barriers to investment participation were stark and systemic. Access to markets was once limited to the affluent, institutional players, or those with extensive networks and education. Even today, persistent structural inequalities and economic disparities shape who feels entitled or empowered to invest. However, the rise of technology, fractional shares, and democratized platforms has radically lowered these thresholds. Yet, psychological and social barriers remain formidable. Many hesitate, believing that their initial sums are insufficient, that the absence of expert credentials disqualifies them, or that the risk of failure warrants abstention. *This subchapter confronts those internal narratives, reframing investment as an inclusive practice, accessible to all who choose to act.*

This shift begins by challenging the myth of the 'ideal investor'—a figure often imagined as wealthy, highly educated, and impeccably successful. Such archetypes create an exclusionary illusion, fostering imposter syndrome among novices and reinforcing economic hierarchies. Psychological research on self-efficacy demonstrates that people's beliefs about their ability to influence outcomes profoundly affect their engagement. Recognising oneself as an investor, even when starting small, catalyses the motivation to learn, persist, and grow. This recognition is less about immediate financial returns and more about claiming a role that shapes one's economic future. *Identity precedes mastery.*

Consider the example of micro-investing platforms that enable users to invest as little as a few pounds. Early adopters often describe a powerful sense of inclusion—not merely transactional participation, but a psychological transformation wherein saving and investing cease to be abstract, intimidating concepts and become tangible, personal practices. This is not incidental but foundational: *the act of investing, no matter the scale, is itself a declaration of ownership over one's financial trajectory.*

Yet, embracing this identity invites tension. Investing involves risk, uncertainty, and the possibility of loss. For many, especially those from historically marginalised communities, these risks carry disproportionate emotional and material weight. The subchapter explores this tension candidly, recognising that 'no longer a bystander' does not imply effortless confidence or unmitigated success. Instead, it entails confronting fear, ambiguity, and systemic constraints with deliberate courage. It is a call to agency that acknowledges context, not a naïve promise of guaranteed prosperity.

Critical to this empowerment is reframing investment as a process rather than a destination. The investor's journey is iterative, marked by learning from setbacks and celebrating incremental progress. This perspective dismantles the binary of success versus failure and replaces it with a continuum of growth and adaptation. It also emphasises that *participation itself generates value*, not only in monetary terms but in knowledge, resilience, and community connection.

Moreover, the democratization of investment demands ethical reflection on the broader societal implications. While individual empowerment is vital, it must coexist with a critique of systems that perpetuate inequality. Recognising oneself as an investor includes a consciousness of how capital circulates and accumulates, and how one's actions contribute to or challenge these patterns. This expanded identity fosters not only personal agency but also social responsibility.

The narrative of 'no longer a bystander' also intersects with cultural and psychological narratives around worthiness and entitlement. The subchapter unpacks how cultural conditioning around money and class influences who feels entitled to participate in investment. It provides tools for readers to dismantle internalised exclusion and reframe financial identity on their own terms. This process is deeply personal and collective, inviting readers to see their engagement as part of a larger movement toward financial inclusion and equity.

Finally, this declaration energises readers to act—not by waiting for external validation or perfect conditions but by recognising that *the moment to claim the role of investor is now*. Practical guidance accompanies this ethos, outlining ways to begin investing with available resources, cultivate financial literacy, and build supportive networks. The subchapter underscores that investing is not a solitary act but a social practice enriched by shared experience and mutual encouragement.

To embrace the investor identity without gatekeeping is to affirm that economic participation is a right, not a privilege. It is to acknowledge that *your agency in financial matters matters.* This subchapter's insights, grounded in research and lived experience, equip readers to step forward confidently, transforming from spectators of the economic system into active participants shaping their own destinies.

Designing a Living Wealth Philosophy:

Designing a living wealth philosophy is an exercise in self-definition that transcends mere financial calculations. It demands a deliberate, thoughtful articulation of values, goals, and behaviours that together compose a coherent framework for managing money, investing, and cultivating prosperity over time. A personal Wealth Manifesto is not a static document but a dynamic compass—a living statement that evolves alongside one's experience, aspirations, and changing circumstances. *Crafting such a manifesto equips readers with clarity and intentionality, anchoring their financial journey in purpose rather than reaction.*

The urgency and significance of this task emerge from a recognition that wealth, in its fullest sense, is not simply an accumulation of assets but a complex interplay of identity, discipline, and meaning. Without a guiding philosophy, investors risk drifting amidst market volatility and societal pressures, susceptible to short-term impulses or the influence of external narratives. A Wealth Manifesto offers a resilient foundation, enabling disciplined action aligned with deeply held principles. This alignment is crucial for maintaining momentum during inevitable setbacks and sustaining motivation through the slow, compound nature of wealth building.

At the core of this process lies the act of introspection. Readers are invited to probe fundamental questions: What does wealth mean to me beyond monetary terms? How do my cultural background, upbringing, and personal experiences shape my relationship with money? What are my non-negotiables in terms of financial ethics and impact? These reflections situate financial choices within a broader life context, connecting the tangible with the intangible. *By integrating emotional and philosophical dimensions into financial planning, the manifesto becomes a holistic tool rather than a sterile budget or investment plan.*

This subchapter proposes a practical template for readers to articulate their Wealth Manifesto. It begins with values identification—encouraging readers to distil the principles that will govern their wealth practice. Examples might include prioritising sustainability, generosity, independence, or legacy. Rather than prescribing universal values, the exercise honours individual diversity and nuance. The manifesto must be authentic to each reader's lived reality and aspirations.

Following values, readers consider defining clear yet flexible financial goals that reflect both ambition and realism. Here, the manifesto bridges vision and action: articulating objectives like building emergency savings, investing regularly, supporting community initiatives, or achieving financial independence within a certain timeframe. *A crucial insight is to frame these goals not as rigid mandates but as evolving targets subject to revision, fostering adaptability and resilience.*

Behavioural commitments constitute the next layer of the manifesto. These are specific practices and habits that embody the philosophy in daily life—setting aside a portion of income for investment, continuing financial education, resisting impulsive spending, or engaging in regular financial reflection. Such commitments reinforce the psychological shift from viewing money management as chore to regarding it as an identity-affirming ritual. The manifesto thus acts as a motivational anchor during moments of fatigue or uncertainty.

The manifesto also incorporates a stance on ethical engagement with wealth. This includes the acknowledgement of one's role in larger economic systems and a commitment to responsible investment or philanthropy. The subchapter emphasises that wealth creation need not be divorced from social consciousness; indeed, embedding ethical considerations enriches the meaning and impact of financial endeavours.

Importantly, the manifesto is framed as a *living document*. Readers are encouraged to revisit and revise it regularly, responding to shifts in life stage, market conditions, or personal growth. This iterative approach prevents stagnation and promotes continuous alignment between evolving identity and financial practice.

Real-world case studies illustrate how individuals across different backgrounds and wealth levels have crafted their Wealth Manifestos, highlighting the diversity of approaches and the transformative effects of intentional design. These narratives demonstrate how the manifesto functions not only as a planning tool but as a source of empowerment and coherence.

Critical reflection is woven throughout, inviting readers to consider potential tensions and challenges. For instance, how to balance aspiration with contentment, or long-term vision with immediate needs. The manifesto is positioned not as a panacea but as a pragmatic strategy to navigate complexity with greater clarity.

Ultimately, designing a living wealth philosophy is an act of self-sovereignty. It reclaims financial agency from the noise of external pressures and fleeting trends, situating the reader as the author of their own economic story. This subchapter equips readers to construct a manifesto that does more than guide money—it shapes identity, nurtures resilience, and sustains a meaningful, enduring engagement with wealth.

Conclusion
Nothing Small About You

Investing modest sums on a limited income is often mischaracterised—not as a deliberate choice but as a concession, a quiet acknowledgement of scarcity rather than an expression of agency. This chapter turns that perception on its head. Small-income investing is not compromise; it is a deliberate reassertion of values. It declares a refusal to be sidelined by conventional economic metrics, redefining wealth itself—not as mere accumulation, but as an embodied practice of identity, resilience, and subtle influence. Here, readers are invited to reconnect with the emotional heart of their financial journey, recognising that steady, modest investment embodies a radical, transformative assertion of self-worth and future potential.

Over the course of this book, we have dismantled the myths that discourage those without abundant resources from entering the investing arena. We have explored psychological barriers, examined practical strategies, and unpacked the cultural narratives that shape our relationship with money. Now, attention turns inward: to what it truly means to live as an investor when resources are limited but intent is expansive. This chapter does more than summarise previous lessons—it elevates them, transforming data and guidance into a philosophy of wealth as a way of being. Wealth, in this sense, is quiet, durable, and deeply personal; it is a daily practice that affirms one's presence within the economic and social fabric, rather than a spectacle of status or excess.

Such a perspective demands an emotional reckoning. Consistently investing small amounts requires patience, faith, and a vision of self that transcends immediate circumstances. It is an act of courage against the pervasive notion that financial success demands grandeur or instant gratification. Readers are encouraged to embrace the paradox of smallness and strength, recognising that incremental contributions can yield profound long-term transformation—both personally and within the communities they inhabit.

The chapter also highlights an often-overlooked dimension: pride in small-scale investing. Many hesitate to adopt the title of 'investor' without reaching conventional benchmarks of wealth or expertise. Yet claiming this identity, regardless of portfolio size, is itself a revolutionary act. It disrupts exclusionary norms and fosters a community where diverse financial realities are acknowledged and respected. Readers are invited to inhabit this role fully, carrying it with confidence and dignity.

A practical, symbolic exercise anchors this reflection: writing a letter to one's future self. This act—postmarked with pride—is both a motivational tool and a marker of identity, linking present efforts to future aspirations in an intimate, tangible form. The letter becomes a personal manifesto, a testament to resilience, vision, and ongoing commitment—a source of encouragement in the face of inevitable challenges.

Philosophically, the chapter situates small-income investing within broader conversations about economic justice, empowerment, and cultural narratives of success. It invites readers to redefine wealth beyond conventional metrics and to honour the quiet revolutions occurring in households, communities, and individual lives. This framing fosters solidarity and collective agency, embedding personal financial growth within a wider social context.

Throughout, the tone balances analytical rigour with compassionate guidance, speaking to readers who seek not merely to understand wealth, but to live it meaningfully. Specificity and nuance prevail over platitude, connecting deeply with universal themes of identity, agency, and hope.

By the chapter's conclusion, readers emerge not only with an intellectual grasp of the significance of their small-scale investing but with a transformed sense of self—a self that recognises the potency of modest, deliberate actions. They are invited to step fully into the role of investor, not as a distant ideal, but as a present reality suffused with quiet power and enduring purpose.

This closing reflection returns to the emotional heart of the book:

The essence of small-income investing transcends mere numbers—it is a profound revolution of values, a quiet yet resolute assertion of agency in a world that often equates financial worth with largesse. This chapter returns to the emotional core of the book, reframing modest investments not as compromises or acts of resignation, but as deliberate, powerful choices that embody resilience and intention. *Small-income investing is, in this light, a declaration: that wealth is not solely about accumulation but about cultivating a way of being—steady, confident, and quietly transformative.* This is a necessary recalibration in financial discourse, one that honours the lived realities of millions while expanding the very definition of economic participation.

Throughout the preceding chapters, readers have navigated the practical terrain of how to save, invest, automate, and develop a personal wealth philosophy on limited means. Yet, all the strategies, tools, and knowledge converge here in an invitation to internalise wealth as a daily attitude and identity. It is a call to recognise that the power of investing lies not only in financial returns but in the ongoing act of self-definition. The process cultivates patience, self-discipline, and a vision anchored not in external validation but in personal conviction. This shift challenges dominant narratives that often marginalise small investors as peripheral or less capable, insisting instead that *every incremental step taken towards financial growth is itself an act of profound courage and transformation.*

Embedded in this reflection is an ethical and philosophical affirmation: wealth as a practice grounded in quiet persistence resists the volatility and spectacle that so often dominate popular conceptions of money. It reframes wealth as a long-term conversation with oneself, one's values, and one's future, rather than a short-lived accumulation of status or consumption. This chapter challenges readers to embrace this ethos fully, to see themselves as architects of enduring change rather than transient participants in a fast-moving economic theatre. The empowerment found in this perspective redefines success, making it accessible and deeply personal.

Central to this closing meditation is a practical, symbolic exercise that crystallises the chapter's theme—a letter to one's future self. This exercise is far more than an abstract gesture; it is a *deliberate act of ownership, a moment of pride that solidifies the reader's role as an investor and steward of their own financial destiny.* Writing to the future self compels a fusion of hope, accountability, and affirmation. It invites readers to articulate not only their aspirations but also the values and lessons they wish to carry forward. The letter becomes a tangible artefact of transformation—something to be revisited, celebrated, and held as a testament to quiet resilience.

This closing exercise embodies a crucial insight: the journey of small-income investing is less about perfection or rapid accumulation and more about sustained, intentional presence. It is about honouring progress, however incremental, and recognising that every effort contributes to a broader, evolving narrative of personal and collective empowerment. In this way, *the reader is invited to cultivate patience with the process, pride in their agency, and an enduring sense of purpose that outlasts market fluctuations or external noise.*

Moreover, this chapter situates the individual's financial journey within wider social and cultural contexts. It acknowledges the structural inequalities that shape access to wealth-building opportunities while affirming the radical potential inherent in claiming financial agency regardless of starting point. By framing small-income investing as a quiet revolution of values, the chapter contributes to a growing discourse on economic inclusion and justice. It stresses that *wealth creation is not merely a personal endeavour but a form of cultural and political resistance against exclusion and erasure.*

The tone throughout balances intellectual rigour with empathetic encouragement, recognising the complexity of emotions—hope, doubt, pride, fear—that accompany financial transformation. It respects the reader's intelligence and lived experience, offering nuanced insights that validate struggles and inspire continued commitment. Each paragraph unfolds with deliberate clarity and a rhythm that sustains engagement while inviting deep reflection.

Readers completing this chapter will carry forward a transformed relationship with wealth—one that transcends conventional metrics to embrace an identity marked by resilience, intentionality, and quiet strength. They will be equipped not only with strategies and knowledge but with a renewed sense of self, ready to approach investing as a continuous, meaningful practice woven into the fabric of daily life. This is wealth as a lived philosophy, as a personal revolution both subtle and profound.

By centring the emotional and ethical dimensions of small-income investing, this chapter offers a definitive closure that honours the reader's journey without reducing it to summary. It calls for a sustained, proud engagement with wealth as a way of being—an enduring legacy crafted not by grand gestures but by the steady accumulation of belief, action, and self-respect. This final reflection stands as both a tribute and a challenge: *to live wealth boldly, humbly, and unapologetically, knowing that nothing small defines your capacity to shape your future.*

About the Author

Leah Wynford writes at the intersection of resilience and resourcefulness. Raised in a working-class household where every dollar mattered, she learned early that wealth isn't just what you accumulate—it's what you believe you're worth. Her work focuses on helping everyday earners transform small incomes into powerful financial agency through psychology, habit design, and human-centered finance. Leah is driven by one question: What if building wealth didn't start with money—but with mindset? Her writing is known for its emotional precision, narrative clarity, and ability to translate complex systems into simple rituals. When she's not writing, she mentors first-generation investors and curates community tools for intentional living.

www.ingramcontent.com/pod-product-compliance
Lightning Source LLC
Chambersburg PA
CBHW031350230926
51848CB00002B/459
9789371773706